"The Elements of Style for the legal pɪ⌐.⌐⌐⌐⌐.. .⌐,.. ⌐⌐⌐ make your legal prose sing."

Clifford W. Gilbert-Lurie, Managing Partner,
Ziffren Brittenham LLP

"An excellent resource for legal writers at all stages of their careers, from law students to experienced litigators. Writing with the elegance that he advocates, McCarl instructs with clear explanations, helpful examples, and practical suggestions. He succeeds in demystifying the art of legal writing."

S. Elizabeth Gibson, Burton Craige Professor of Law Emerita,
University of North Carolina School of Law

"Keep McCarl's tips in mind and judges will read your briefs with appreciation rather than frustration—which in turn makes for more auspicious oral arguments and results."

Tim Kowal, appellate attorney and co-host of the
California Appellate Law Podcast

Elegant Legal Writing

Elegant Legal Writing

Ryan McCarl

UNIVERSITY OF CALIFORNIA PRESS

University of California Press
Oakland, California

Library of Congress Cataloging-in-Publication Data

Names: McCarl, Ryan Patrick, 1985– author.
Title: Elegant legal writing / Ryan McCarl.
Description: First. | Oakland : University of California Press, 2024. |
    Includes bibliographical references and index.
Identifiers: LCCN 2023016750 (print) | LCCN 2023016751 (ebook) |
    ISBN 9780520395787 (cloth) | ISBN 9780520395794 (paperback) |
    ISBN 9780520395800 (ebook)
Subjects: LCSH: Legal composition.
Classification: LCC KF250 .M375 2024 (print) | LCC KF250 (ebook) |
    DDC 808.06/634—dc23/eng/20230712
LC record available at https://lccn.loc.gov/2023016750
LC ebook record available at https://lccn.loc.gov/2023016751

32 31 30 29 28 27 26 25 24 23
10 9 8 7 6 5 4 3 2 1

To my grandparents

Contents

Expanded Contents

Acknowledgments

Publishing a book has been my lifelong ambition, and I am grateful beyond words to everyone who has helped me along the way. There are too many to mention, even if I limit myself to thanking those who helped me bring the manuscript across the finish line after it was accepted.

My wife Nora's love, support, and companionship make everything I do possible. My colleagues at Rushing McCarl LLP—John Rushing, Carol Risher, and Davit Avagyan—put more on their shoulders so I could step away from the day-to-day pressures of legal practice for long enough to finish this project. My cat Plato kept me company and lay down on my keyboard whenever I ignored him for too long, just as he has since law school. You can blame him for any typos.

I've also received generous feedback from many editors and reviewers, especially Michael Hui, Brenda Matlack, Gayle Ito-Hamerling, Matthew Cavedon, Ross Guberman, Paisley Shoemaker, Geoffrey Gilbert, Frances K. Browne, and my editors at the University of California Press.

·　·　·　·　·

I have always known that I would dedicate my first book to my grandparents. They made me believe that I could do whatever I wanted with my life, even though the options available to me were never available to them.

Grandpa Moblo worked in a factory for decades before retiring with a pension when I was a toddler. When I turned six and decided to build a robot, he took me to the library to borrow books on robotics. When I turned eleven and decided to learn to program, he gave me a job so I could earn money to buy my first computer. When I turned thirteen and decided to learn Japanese, he and Grandma Moblo took me to Barnes & Noble and bought me a $25 book-and-CD course that led to a study-abroad scholarship a few years later.

Most Monday evenings in high school, Grandpa and I would go to Cheapstacks, a bookstore in Grand Haven that sold used books for $5 a bag, and I hauled home hundreds of books on any subject that caught my interest. Flipping through these books over the years introduced me to countless ideas that shaped my thinking.

I was lucky to have a family that encouraged my love of language and literature. No one told me to stop writing poetry and pick a practical major, that reading philosophy was pointless, or that my op-eds for the school newspaper could interfere with future job searches. If I was told such things, I didn't listen, because my family gave me the confidence to brush off discouragement and pursue my always-changing goals.

Thanks largely to their love and support, I found my way to a life where I can learn, teach, and advocate for a living, and use my love of language to help my clients and elevate my profession. My first book is for them.

Introduction

Writing briefs that persuade and impress judges is no easy task. Most judges are overwhelmed with work and can't afford to spend more time than needed with the filings that cross their desks. But a client's litigation goals often depend on their attorney's ability to get a judge's attention and make concise, compelling arguments.

Reading legal documents should be painless. Upon opening a litigation brief, a judge should be able to immediately perceive its main arguments, then experience a sense of relief upon discovering that it includes a lucid, accurate, and easy-to-follow explanation of the relevant facts and law.

Three core principles underlie *Elegant Legal Writing*:

1. **Readability**. Judges and clients have limited time, attention span, and motivation to read legal documents. Attorneys should therefore cultivate a style that is concise and easy to read.

2. **Simplicity**. Legal writers should reduce complexity whenever possible, giving readers only the details they need.

3. **Aesthetics**. Attorneys should cultivate their ear for language and aim to write engaging and pleasant prose.

The word *elegance,* defined by the *Oxford English Dictionary* as "harmonious simplicity and tasteful appropriateness in the choice and arrangement of words," captures these values.

This book collects insights and techniques that have resonated with me and my students. I've shared these lessons in continuing legal education seminars and writing courses at the UCLA School of Law and the LMU Loyola Law School, and I use them daily in my litigation practice. While mainly offering practical guidance for attorneys and law students—with chapters 7 through 9 relating specifically to litigation—*Elegant Legal Writing* can help anyone who writes for professional audiences.

Attorneys who write well project an image of expertise and win more cases. Studying prose techniques will make you a better advocate.

PART I Style

1 Core Principles of Legal Writing

Lawyers should strive to write documents that are clear, easy to understand, and enjoyable to read. Lucid legal writing can lead readers to forget that they are reading for work instead of pleasure.

1.1. Adopt a growth mindset.

The way you think about writing and learning will influence how much value you gain from activities such as reading this book, taking legal writing seminars, or receiving detailed feedback on a draft. Psychologist Carol Dweck used the term *growth mindset* to describe a set of positive beliefs that make learners more resilient and open to new ideas.[1] This section discusses three beliefs that can put you in the right frame of mind to improve your writing skills.

Belief no. 1: Studying writing is a worthwhile use of your time.

Identify why writing skills matter to you. If you believe that improving your writing will make you a better lawyer and help you obtain better outcomes for your clients, for example, then you'll be more receptive to feedback and new ideas.

For lawyers, writing is not just one skill among others, on the same footing as questioning techniques, substantive legal expertise, or negotiation savvy. Although a few attorneys may be so good at trial advocacy that no one cares whether they can write, such cases are rare. Most legal work consists of *written* communication and advocacy, so the ability to write competently is a prerequisite to success as a lawyer. Attorneys who go further—who learn to write artfully and persuasively—can earn professional respect unavailable to most peers and competitors.

Belief no. 2: However strong your writing, you can always improve.

Most attorneys, because of self-selection and years of education, already have the language background, intellect, and knowledge to write at least passable legal prose. Many are strong writers who still have room to grow, while others need to improve more than they realize.

Although attorneys should write with a sense of confidence, don't allow your ego to make you resist feedback and miss out on learning opportunities. Working to improve as a writer is analogous to learning a musical instrument: there is no finish line. If writing well matters to you, strive to get better at it every week.

Belief no. 3: Writing skills can be taught and learned.

Writing is too often spoken of as an innate ability rather than a set of skills that can be studied and practiced.

Skilled writers draw on their writing experience, knowledge of technique, sense of rhythm and sound, empathy with the audience, experience telling and listening to stories, and intuition for language as honed by years of reading. All these can be cultivated. The techniques that make some legal briefs more readable and persuasive than others can be taught, as this book shows.

1.2. Commit to improving your writing skills.

There are four main ways to improve as a writer: studying writing craft, reading widely, practicing often, and seeking feedback.

Study writing craft.

Legal writing courses usually focus on research and brief structure rather than prose style, so many lawyers never study composition principles like those taught in this book.

You can seek out opportunities to learn more about writing by attending continuing legal education classes, hiring an editor or writing coach, and reading books like this one. Law firms should integrate writing instruction into their practice by bringing in writing experts to give seminars, hiring editors and writing coaches, encouraging candid feedback, and otherwise investing in their attorneys' writing skills.

Read widely and often, with an eye toward style as well as substance.

Read widely to tune your ear for language. Don't restrict yourself to legal materials; make time for literature and general nonfiction, too. Although it's not easy for attorneys to make time for pleasure reading, it may help to see reading time as a way to refresh your mind and improve your writing skills by exposing yourself to fresh language, new ideas, and unfamiliar vocabulary.

Consider subscribing to sophisticated generalist publications about politics, arts, and culture—outlets such as *The New Yorker*, *The Economist*, *Harper's*, *The New York Review of Books*, and *The Atlantic*. For contemporary literature, I recommend *The Paris Review* and *Poetry*; for daily news, *The New York Times*. These periodicals cater to highly educated readers, so they hire the best writers and editors they can find, and their articles usually show a painstaking attention to language and style.

Reading literature, even by listening to audiobooks, will improve how you think and write. Literary works, classic or contemporary, have been thoroughly edited. Their writers have scrutinized every paragraph, sentence, and word with an eye toward such matters as rhythm and imagery. Think about their choices and allow them to develop your sensitivity to language.

Train yourself to read with an eye to both content and style, attending to not just what is being said but how the writer says it. Notice what you like and dislike about different styles and consider how you might use the techniques you observe. When reading an article that aims to persuade, try to understand the rhetorical and argumentative moves the writer makes.

See writing tasks as opportunities for deliberate practice.

Writing well requires practice. In general, the best writers are those who regularly devote significant amounts of time to writing. Also, each time you perform a particular type of writing task (drafting discovery requests or a complaint, for example) you'll get better and faster at that task.

Psychologist Anders Ericsson argued that expertise is built through deliberate practice.[2] One becomes a better writer by writing a lot while consciously working to improve one's craft. You can think of each writing task as an instance of "practice" that will, if deliberately performed and closely attended to, help you improve as a writer.

When you finish a project, don't put it away immediately; instead, reflect on what you could have improved about the document or your writing process. Compare early drafts to the final version to make yourself more aware of areas for improvement and note these for future reference.

Seek out editing and feedback.

Many lawyers dread feedback. Some see extensive edits as a personal criticism of their lawyering and attention to detail. This sensitivity is understandable given the centrality of writing in legal practice; it is hard to be both a poor writer and a good lawyer. And for associate attorneys in their first few years out of law school, eager to meet a firm's expectations, it can be hard to see a supervisor's extensive edits as something other than a message of displeasure with the quality of the associate's work.

But to improve as a writer, you must overcome any aversion you feel toward editing. A good editor's suggestions say something about the draft, not its author.

When law firms make candid feedback and thorough editing standard practices, attorneys are more likely to see colleagues' edits as a routine and nonthreatening step in the firm's quality-control procedures.

1.3. Aim to write prose that is clear, readable, and efficient.

> Whoever knows he is deep strives for clarity; whoever would
> like to appear deep to the crowd, strives for obscurity.
> —Friedrich Nietzsche, *The Gay Science*

Despite decades of effort by legal-writing experts, there remains a misconception that legal writing should be difficult to read. Lawyers tend to adopt the language of their community. Law school introduces legal Latinisms (e.g., *arguendo*), redundant doublets (e.g., *terms and conditions*), and circumlocutions (e.g., *the above-captioned case*) to students, who then use these devices in their own drafts. At first the legalese bolsters the new lawyer's self-identity as a member of an impressive profession, and then its use becomes an unconscious habit.

Some lawyers believe that legal prose must be complex because the law is complex, but the opposite is true. A lawyer's job is to chart a path through complexity—not add barriers to understanding.

The three related concepts of *clarity, readability,* and *efficiency* are the main virtues that distinguish a strong legal prose style. *Clarity* refers to how well the text conveys your intended meaning. *Readability* refers to how easy it is to read and parse the text. *Efficiency* refers to how much relevant information the text conveys in proportion to its length and difficulty.

Other stylistic defects—awkward idioms, clumsy rhythms, and so on—will be forgiven if the text is clear and easy to read. Additionally, style, substance, and persuasion are intertwined. A clear prose style correlates with clear thought.

Many lawyers resist this advice. Some confuse legalese with specialized "terms of art," which carry an established meaning that is cumbersome to express in ordinary language. Or they fear that modernizing the boiler-plate language used by their predecessors might put their clients at risk. It feels safer to stick with tradition.

But stylists and legal-writing scholars advocate a plain-language style that is, as Jacques Barzun put it, "simple and direct." Given their unanimity, one would expect the plain-language style to be the norm in legal writing, but that is not the case. Although plain-language principles are increasingly evident in briefs filed by litigators at elite firms, most legal writing remains turgid, boring, and painful to read. It need not be so.

1.4. Learn the principles of readability.

Almost all the tips and strategies in this book aim to make your legal prose more readable. Unnecessarily complex prose taxes the reader's memory, attention span, and motivation, so it's less likely to be carefully read or understood. Judges can be persuaded only by arguments they understand.

This section describes some high-level concepts associated with readability.[3] Even a passing familiarity with these will help you absorb this book's recommendations and develop them into automatic reflexes.

Some texts are more readable than others, requiring less exertion from the reader while conveying similar information, because they impose less of a burden on the reader's attention and short-term memory. Unnecessarily complex prose imposes a greater cognitive burden on the reader.

All readers have limited time, energy, attention span, and appetite for obligatory reading. These constraints are especially acute for trial-court judges, who must distribute their scarce time and energy across all the active cases in their dockets.

Along with extrinsic constraints such as limited time, all readers have cognitive constraints that limit their ability to process written text. Here are some concepts to know:

Working memory. The reader's understanding of a sentence depends on the context created by the preceding text, some of which the reader holds in their working memory. A reader's working memory can only hold about five linguistic "objects" at once. If the writer takes too long to complete a thought, they may lose the reader before conveying the intended meaning.

Attention span and motivation. Readers are more likely to understand and remember something they read if the writer sets out to be useful and makes their point before the reader's attention drifts. Relatedly, if a judge senses that your brief will not help them reach a sound conclusion, they may stop reading.

Task-switching. Readers can focus on only one stimulus or processing task at a time. There is no such thing as multitasking, only rapid switching between tasks. Switching focus from one processing task to another has imperceptible cognitive costs; it slows readers down and interferes with comprehension. Inefficient task-switching occurs when the reader loses track of what the document is talking about and must backtrack.

Integrating information and resolving uncertainty. When confronted with new information, readers try to integrate it into what they already know. Relatedly, readers try to resolve uncertainties as quickly as possible. This applies to macro-level tasks, such as grasping an argument, and micro-level tasks, such as identifying what a pronoun refers to.

The scarce resources of attention, energy, and motivation are interrelated. They play a central role in determining whether your brief successfully conveys your argument to an overworked reader.

1.5. Distinguish rules from guidelines.

Most writing advice should be prefaced with the qualifier "all else equal." All else equal, for example, shorter words and sentences are more efficient than longer words and sentences. Active-voice constructions make for livelier prose than passive-voice constructions. Palatino Linotype is a more readable font than Times New Roman.

But other considerations often warrant a departure from these guidelines. Perhaps your local judge mandates that briefs use the typewriter-style font Courier or some other design blunder. You'll have to follow court rules. (If such a misguided edict comes from your supervising partner instead of a judge, send them a copy of this book.)

Some lawyers resist writing advice on the theory that what constitutes good prose is a matter of personal preference. They once learned that two spaces after a period are better than one, so they "disagree" with the advice to use one space. Their high-school teachers told them to never split infinitives, so they think this sentence contains a grammar error. Their first bosses after law school made them write headings in all-caps, and they'll do so until they retire.

These mindsets are just forms of resistance to learning something new. Most writing and design experts agree there should be only one space between sentences, so it's indefensible to stick with the two-space approach unless you have reason to believe that the experts are wrong.[4]

Writing advice occupies a spectrum. On one end, there are established prescriptive rules that ought not to be broken; on the other, there are matters debated by experts who study prose for a living. If you're unsure where along that spectrum a recommendation falls, here is a test: can you find a writing stylist who espouses the opposite view?

Composition is a craft, not a free-for-all in which all opinions hold equal weight, so books about style often have overlapping recommendations. This book's guidelines about writing mechanics align with those of other stylists and with the "plain-language" philosophy that legal-writing professors have promoted for decades. When I disagree with widespread advice, as I do with respect to footnotes,[5] I note those disagreements so the reader can consider other approaches.

Composition is also an art. There are an infinite number of variables that can influence how a writer expresses a thought. Most writing advice is therefore necessarily tentative and general. It is ideally rooted in a combination of expert opinion, readability studies, principles of logic and design, and intuition shaped by a lifetime of reading and writing.

1.6. Balance competing values in writing tasks.

Writing guidelines often conflict, requiring the writer to evaluate tradeoffs and choose between different ways of expressing the same idea. This process can be guided by a sense of how to prioritize the values underlying different pieces of advice.

If you're writing a discovery motion, you'll have different priorities than someone writing a poem. Aesthetic considerations, such as pace and rhythm, matter even in litigation writing, but they are less important than complying with court rules and making the judge's job easier by using a plain-language style.

Here is a suggested ranking of values for litigation writing:

1. Fulfilling your ethical duties (including the duties to be competent, to avoid misstating the facts or law, and to avoid misleading the tribunal).

2. Filing the document on time.

3. Following the court's rules so the clerk doesn't reject your filing and you don't lose the motion on a technicality.

4. Clearly explaining your point.

5. Persuasively arguing your point.

6. Avoiding blunders (such as spelling and grammar errors).

7. Making the filing as short and readable as possible.

8. Holding the reader's interest and motivating the reader to continue.

9. Making the text pleasant to read by using effective style techniques.

10. Making the text appear professional and impressive by following sound layout, design, and citation-formatting practices.

For other forms of legal writing—most notably, contracts and statutes—the need to avoid ambiguity and rule out competing interpretations often overrides other values.

1.7. Include only relevant details and put them in context.

Context is critical in writing. The advice to "write as you speak" is unhelpful because spoken interactions occur in a live social context. That context lends meaning to vague and nonverbal expressions, helps resolve ambiguous references (that is, makes clear what someone is talking about), and creates an atmosphere of shared meaning.

Written documents, by contrast, usually need to provide context.[6] Once the writer provides a context—a mental world they invite the reader into—they can leave more to implication and rely more on the reader's cooperation.

Context gives meaning to details, determines their importance, and shows how they interrelate. Your document should include only details that matter, and those details' relevance should be made clear. A reader should never be left to guess how details fit into a conceptual structure and work together to convey meaning, tell a story, or make an argument.

1.8. Motivate readers by showing how your document will help them.

Motivation is a critical determinant of a reader's attention span. We pay more attention to text that strikes us as interesting and relevant to our purposes.

Most readers, when they pick up an unfamiliar document, subconsciously ask themselves: "Why should I spend time reading this?" This is especially true of busy readers such as lawyers and judges. You need to reassure these readers immediately that they should invest their time and energy in your document.

To do so, try to see the text from the reader's perspective and think about the problem they need to solve. At the start of the document, show that you understand that problem, tell the reader what solution you've found, and provide a roadmap that previews the most important reasons your solution is correct.

1.9. Think like a teacher.

To put yourself in the right frame of mind for legal writing, it helps to think of yourself not just as an advocate but as a teacher. In a risk-analysis letter, you teach the client the information they need to make an informed decision about how to handle a legal matter. In a motion, you teach the judge the rules and analytical moves that, when applied to the relevant facts, lead to the conclusion that your motion should be granted.

No one is likely to be persuaded by a text or argument they do not understand, so you must impose order on the raw material of your case—the applicable law, facts, and record—to help the judge grasp the parts that matter. Only then will you be ready to persuade.

Legal documents should adjust to the reader's background knowledge. In general, assume that your reader is a well-informed member of the legal community who is a bit rusty on the specific topics you are covering. Don't waste the reader's time with information they already know.

Here's an example, from an appellate brief, of what to avoid:

Standard of Review
The "standard of review" refers to how the appellate court conducts its examination of the matter on appeal. *Morrison,* 538 Pa. at 131.

Every appellate judge knows what a standard of review is. You should say which standard applies in your case (e.g., abuse of discretion or clear error), but you don't need to explain the concept of a standard of review.

1.10. Avoid common audience-related mistakes.

Writing with your audience's needs in mind can help you avoid some bad habits that abound in legal writing:

Avoid research dumps. If you're writing a brief or memo, don't try to include everything you learned while researching. Judges, colleagues, and clients want you to clear a path through the thicket of the law, not reproduce that thicket in your document.[7] The point of a legal document is never to show how hard you've worked to solve a problem. Rather, the point is the conclusion you've reached and the reasons supporting the conclusion.

Don't snipe at opponents. Lawyers often pepper their filings with snarky asides and sniping at the opposing party or its lawyers. Avoid this practice. A judge reading your brief wants to know why they should grant or deny the relief requested. Judges are not interested in petty grievances between opposing counsel.

Avoid unnecessary legal-history lessons. Most legal audiences are eager for you to get to the point, so they are rarely interested in how a doctrine became the law. Just say what the law is, not how it came to be—unless your opponent relies on outdated law, or you have one of the unusual cases in which a court needs to understand a doctrine's history to decide the case properly.

2 Concision

2.1. Omit throat-clearing introductory phrases.

2.2. Delete unnecessary modifiers, especially intensifiers.

2.3. Avoid overspecification and synonym strings.

2.4. Avoid doublets and triplets.

2.5. Condense bloated phrases.

If an idea can be communicated equally well in two ways, lawyers should choose the more concise way unless they have a good reason to do otherwise.

Litigation briefs usually have page limits. Baggy writing occurs when lawyers fill pages not with incisive arguments that make the most of an opportunity to persuade, but with nonsense and sludge.

Lest you fear that pursuing concision will make your briefs choppy, remember that concision is just one characteristic of effective prose; it is one value that must sometimes be sacrificed for others. But no readers will complain that your document is too short or your sentences too tight.

All else equal, shorter sentences, paragraphs, and documents are easier to read. Although adding words and sentences can sometimes make a text more readable by providing helpful details or showing each step in a chain of reasoning, question whether each phrase and sentence contributes to the reader's understanding. Delete text that does not convey important information or serve some other reader-oriented purpose.

First drafts normally overflow with redundant text. In legal briefs, this redundancy can take many forms—ritual phrases (e.g., "Plaintiff respectfully requests that . . ."), unnecessary second or third citations for uncontested propositions, lazy block quotations, lengthy explanations of points the judge already knows, and so on. We will discuss such problems throughout this book.

Discarding clutter from your sentences allows you to communicate the same idea faster, giving the reader a more direct route to their goal. Since judges read briefs for duty rather than pleasure, they will appreciate your consideration for their time. Fluff-free sentences also make your prose more pleasant to read because they improve rhythm.

This chapter offers strategies to tighten your prose and make it more efficient. If you learn to see the words and phrases you can routinely delete or condense, you'll be better able to focus on challenges like coherence, organization, rhythm, and persuasion.

Line editing for concision is the easiest part of writing to teach and learn.[1] Bloated phrases and redundancies often follow patterns that are worth memorizing so that you can recognize and correct them immediately.

2.1. Omit throat-clearing introductory phrases.

Throat-clearing phrases (also known as wind-up phrases) force the reader to wade through meaningless introductory text before the author reveals a sentence's substance. Many such phrases end with the word *that* or a comma. Delete these whenever they occur:

- As a matter of fact . . .
- At the end of the day . . .
- In the final analysis . . .
- It goes without saying that . . .
- It is apparent/clear/essential that . . .
- It is directed that . . .
- It is important to keep in mind that . . .
- It is important to note/recognize that . . .
- It is respectfully suggested that . . .
- It might be said that . . .

- It should be noted that . . .
- It would appear that . . .
- Keep in mind that . . .
- Needless to say . . .
- Plaintiff respectfully submits/requests that . . .

These are just examples. Question every sentence and phrase to ensure that it adds information the reader needs.

2.2. Delete unnecessary modifiers, especially intensifiers.

Legal writing is commonly peppered with unnecessary modifiers (adverbs, adjectives, and phrases acting as such). There is nothing inherently wrong with modifiers; indeed, they are often essential. But as with any words and phrases, modifiers are justified only if they add valuable detail, substance, or clarity. When in doubt, omit them.

The following subsections discuss often-unnecessary *intensifiers* as well as modifiers that convey little information or are redundant.

Intensifiers

Intensifiers are words and phrases like *clearly*, *unquestionably*, and *beyond doubt* that aim to artificially strengthen whatever they modify. Here are some intensifiers to consider revising or omitting:

- basic
- certainly
- clearly
- completely
- enormously
- extremely
- fundamentally
- highly

- indeed
- it is clear that
- literally
- merely
- obviously
- significantly
- squarely
- thoroughly
- totally
- unquestionably
- utter/utterly
- very
- whatsoever
- wholly

Intensifiers seldom communicate additional information, but superfluity is not the worst of their vices. They may make your writing sound strident or hyperbolic. Hyperbolic writing overstates the strength of one's argument or the weakness of an opponent's argument, risking the writer's credibility.

As an extreme example, one litigant used the intensifier *utterly* fifty-five times in a single filing, with statements like the following:

> Defendant's original response was **completely** nonresponsive, **utterly** ignoring the gravamen of the RFAs.

> Defendant's motion is **utterly** confusing and ignores Plaintiff's discovery responses.

Legal readers are trained to be skeptical. Intensifiers have a "because I said so" quality that often causes them to backfire and make an assertion *less* convincing than it would be without the intensifier. They tend to trigger reflexive defenses in the reader's mind.

This is so because intensifiers commonly appear in statements that lawyers call *conclusory*. Conclusory statements assert a conclusion without giving reasons for the conclusion. In legal writing, any debatable proposition must be supported by reasons such as citations to authority. A statement that the defendant's actions were "clearly unreasonable" needs backing; the word *clearly* does not provide such backing.

Here are some excerpts from litigation filings with modifiers that should be discarded:

> The provisions enacted in the Act are not at issue **in the above-captioned case** because the provisions in subtitle C were permanent upon enactment and did not contain a sunset provision.

> Borrower may pay this Note's principal or accrued interest (or both) **in whole or in part** at any time before the Maturity Date.

> That case **expressly** stands for the proposition that a zoning ordinance which **merely** decreased the market value of property does not necessarily violate constitutional provisions forbidding uncompensated takings.

> The bank **obviously** did not become entitled to the gross amount of the subcontract price.

> The damage was caused by actions of public employees having no relation to the function of a public improvement **whatsoever**.

Empty modifiers

Some modifiers can be deleted because they add little or no information to your sentence. Try deleting these:

- actual/actually
- express/expressly
- given
- important
- meaningful/meaningfully
- respective/respectively
- specifically
- virtually

Redundant modifiers

Some modifiers are redundant because they describe traits inherent in the term they are modifying. Here are a few examples:

- advance planning
- briefly summarize
- close proximity
- completely destroyed
- entirely omitted
- expressly written
- false misrepresentation
- harmful injuries
- past experience
- quietly whispered
- regular routine
- secretly concealed
- serious danger
- specifically stated
- subtle tweak
- true facts
- unexpected emergency
- usual habit

Duplicative modifiers

Redundancy also occurs when writers use several descriptive modifiers where one would do, either because the descriptors are synonymous or because one encompasses the other. While revising this book, I noticed my own tendency to use parallel constructions with duplicative modifiers:

Advocate **fairly and with integrity.**

The same habit can crop up when one uses two nouns where one will do:

> The **advice and recommendations** in this book will make your writing more efficient.

> Writers should minimize **jargon and unnecessary technical vocabulary**.

Or two verbs where one will do:

> Lawyers should **understand and watch for** these forms of indeterminacy.

The instruction to *watch for* an error presupposes that the reader understands what to watch for.

2.3. Avoid overspecification and synonym strings.

Lawyers often use strings of synonyms and near-synonyms to make a statement cover every conceivable contingency. Although this practice may be defensible in the context of contracts or discovery requests, it is rarely justified in litigation filings. In any context, avoid reflexively enumerating examples or synonyms; have a reason for every word you include.

Consider the following sentence from a complaint:

> Ponce never gave permission, or assigned, licensed, or otherwise consented to Defendants using or altering her image, likeness, or identity to advertise, promote, market, or endorse Defendants' business, the Club, or any Club event.

Some concepts in this sentence are duplicative synonyms (e.g., *gave permission* and *consented, promote* and *market*). Others encompass each other (e.g., licensing and assigning are ways to give consent). If Ponce didn't consent to the defendants' use of her image, then she must have not assigned or licensed the image to them. Here's a revision:

> Ponce never agreed that Defendants may use her name, image, or likeness to promote their business.

Here's another example, this one from a jury instruction:

> If you find that any one or more of these seven ("7") statements has not been proved, then your verdict must be for the defendant.

Any one or more should be replaced with *any*, and *seven ("7")* should be replaced with *seven*. Here's a revision that also makes the instruction more readable by switching the second half of the sentence to active voice:

> If you find that any of these seven statements have not been proved, then you must return a verdict for the defendant.

Besides making prose less readable, overspecification can backfire by implicitly limiting the generality of certain terms. This is because of the *ejusdem generis* interpretation principle. If an enumeration of items is followed by general words, the general words may be held to apply only to items similar to those specifically mentioned.[2] For example:

- An obstruction-of-justice statute criminalizing the concealment or destruction of "any record, document, or tangible object" was held not to encompass the defendant's destruction of illegally caught fish.[3]
- A discovery request seeking "documents, receipts, memoranda, notations, and other records" might be held not to encompass audio recordings.
- A will devising "my furniture, clothes, cooking utensils, motor vehicles, and other property" might be held not to encompass real estate.

2.4. Avoid doublets and triplets.

Doublets and triplets are set phrases consisting of two or three synonyms.[4] These are common in legal writing. Revise them whenever one or more of the synonyms in the phrase is superfluous, as in the following phrases:

- agree and covenant → agree
- aid and abet → aid
- any and all → all, any
- cancel, annul, and set aside → cancel
- cease and desist → stop, cease
- due and owing/payable → due
- each and every → every, each

- free and clear → free, clear
- make and enter into → make
- null and void → void
- over and above → above
- rules and regulations → rules, regulations
- terms and conditions → terms
- true and correct → true

Here are some examples in litigation documents (doublets and triplets in bold):

> The term *all* with reference to the term *document* means **any and all, each and every** such document as that term is defined.

> In conjunction with the parties' Stipulation of Dismissal and Stay (filed concurrently herewith), Plaintiffs Breyer AG and Breyer Inc. hereby **state, agree, and covenant** as follows.

> SUDESH SINGH AND SURENDER K. SINGH, the undersigned grantors, for a valuable consideration, receipt of which is hereby acknowledged, do hereby **remise, release, and forever quitclaim** to SINGH LIVING TRUST the following described real property in the City of Sacramento, County of Sacramento, State of California.

2.5. Condense bloated phrases.

A *phrase* is a portion of a sentence that makes sense as a unit but lacks a subject or verb (or both). Look for opportunities to condense phrases, communicating the same information in fewer words. Here's a revisable example:

> The successor agency **is obligated to** transfer the appropriate amounts to the county auditor-controller for distribution to the taxing entities.

Suggested revision:

> The successor agency **must** transfer the appropriate amounts to the county auditor-controller for distribution to the taxing entities.

Here are some common phrase structures that can be condensed.[5]

Condensable verb phrases

- deemed required → required
- enter into an agreement → agree
- have an effect → affect
- have knowledge of → know
- hold the belief that → believe
- is dependent on → depends on
- is violative of → violates
- make a distinction → distinguish
- make an assumption → assume
- perform an evaluation → evaluate
- provide an explanation of → explain
- put pressure on → pressure

Noun phrases replaceable with gerunds (-ing words)

Example: *The development of the new rules took three years.* → *Developing the new rules took three years.*

- the inclusion of → including
- the investigation of → investigating
- the maintenance of → maintaining
- the negotiation of → negotiating

Not-*phrases and double negatives*

- do not agree → disagree
- do not have a right to → may not
- not available → unavailable

- not capable → incapable
- not certain → uncertain
- not less than → at least
- not unhelpful → helpful
- not unlike → like
- will not be able to → will be unable to

Bloated or unnecessary prepositional phrases

Check every prepositional phrase to ensure that you have been as concise as possible. One easy fix is to replace *of*-phrases with possessives whenever you can:

> the behavior of the plaintiff → the plaintiff's behavior
>
> the opinion of the expert → the expert's opinion

Check whether the prepositional phrase can be omitted, as in the following examples.

> The Court has already determined that issue **in this case**. [In litigation filings, attorneys are assumed to be writing about the present case, and not some other case, unless they specify otherwise.]
>
> Defendant contends **in his opposition brief** that . . . [The argument's location is likely insignificant or obvious from the context.]

Here are other prepositional phrases to revise:

- at any time → anytime
- at this point in time → now, currently
- despite the fact that → although, while
- during such time as → while, during
- for the price of $100 → for $100
- for the purpose of → to
- for the reason that → because
- in accordance with → according to

- in connection with → about
- in spite of the fact that → although
- in the near future → soon, shortly
- on a regular basis → regularly, routinely
- on numerous occasions → often
- over the duration of → during, throughout
- period of time → time, period
- the majority of → most
- until such time as → until
- with regard to → about, regarding
- with the exception of → except for, besides

By the way, the common adage that says to avoid ending a sentence with a preposition is misleading. It is true that well-written sentences often end on a word that carries meaning, rather than one that serves a purely grammatical function, because the last word in a sentence normally receives the most emphasis. Even so, there is nothing wrong with sentences such as these:

Whom did you give the document to?

It's not clear what that device is used for.

Trust your ear and choose the most natural formulation for what you mean to say. Over time, improve your ear by reading as much well-written prose as you can.

3 Plain Language

The previous chapter showed you ways to tighten your sentences by deleting words and condensing phrases. This chapter introduces other principles of plain-language style that make prose easier to read.

3.1. Understand how word choice affects readability.

Most stylists agree that professional documents should be written in plain language, minimizing jargon. Prose that uses familiar words is more readable than prose that uses uncommon words or abbreviations.

Plain language makes text easier to read for many reasons. One is that years of exposure to common words prepare readers to recognize and process those words. Another is that common words tend to fulfill the reader's unconscious expectations. As the reader progresses from sentence to sentence, their mind predicts that the next clause or phrase will contain common words.

Unexpected text, such as a rare word, interrupts the reader's flow by causing them to pause and notice the oddity, shifting their focus away from the document's substance. These pauses add up quickly; each is an obstacle between the reader and their goals.

Concrete language, abstraction, and visualization

Sentences about abstract concepts are harder to read than sentences about people and tangible objects. It is easier for readers to imagine, reason about, and remember visual images than words or ideas. That is why many mnemonic systems involve associating abstractions such as numbers (e.g., "420737") with specific images (e.g., "passengers using cannabis on a jumbo jet"). Visual images lighten readers' cognitive load by reducing the information they must store in working memory.[1]

Vague terms also make it harder to grasp the author's meaning.[2] Some theorists have described the act of reading as a repeating cycle in which the reader makes predictions about the next clause or sentence, then narrows the set of possible meanings as new text is processed. Easy-to-read texts do not leave readers in prolonged uncertainty about what the author is saying.

Abstractions are unavoidable in legal writing; the law is a network of abstract rules that govern human interactions. But that makes it even more important to write clearly and say what you mean.

3.2. Learn and apply the principles of plain-language style.

A key aspect of writing style is diction (word selection). Use the word that most precisely communicates your meaning, but if several words are equally suitable, your default choice should be the simplest word available. The best legal writers cultivate a plain-language style that is, as stylist Jacques Barzun put it, "simple and direct."

To that end, delete unnecessary words, and follow these guidelines in choosing the words you keep:[3]

- Prefer short words.
- Prefer concrete and specific words.
- Prefer familiar words.
- Prefer singular nouns.
- Prefer words to symbols, initials, and abbreviations.
- Prefer English words and phrases to Latinisms.

These and other principles are discussed in the sections that follow. Internalizing them will make your documents easier and more pleasant to read.

3.3. Avoid legalese and ritual phrases.

Legal writing abounds with sentences that only a lawyer could write. Consider this example (from a demand letter):

> The undersigned hereby further notifies you and each of you that he does not recognize any right alleged by you, whether referred to by you in said lease or not, to the return to you of Twenty Thousand Dollars ($20,000) or any sum at all, as alleged in your notice of intention to terminate said lease, or for any reason, right, or claim whatsoever, and on the contrary, hereby notifies you that pursuant to Paragraph 10 of said Rex Arms lease, upon the final termination of said lease by you, pursuant to your notice of intention to terminate said lease, you and each of you shall and will thereupon forfeit all of your right, title and interest in and to said Twenty-Five Thousand Dollars ($25,000) and/or Twenty Thousand Dollars ($20,000) or any and all sums referred to therein, to the undersigned.

That paragraph was written in the 1940s, but many of its linguistic devices—such as the repetition of numbers, pompous references to *the undersigned*, and use of jargon such as *said lease* and *therein*—remain common. These devices are perpetuated by each generation of law graduates, many of whom are inclined to play it safe by sticking to timeworn incantations used by their predecessors.

Rather than trying to sound like a lawyer, try to sound like a writer of popular nonfiction. Your role is to explain complex ideas in a clear, simple, and persuasive way.

Jargon is abstract technical or pseudo-technical language that professionals use to communicate among themselves and mark themselves as insiders. Jargon often leaks into nonspecialist language as well, as one sees in the spread of such terms as *utilize* or *leverage* (instead of *use*), *impact* (instead of the verb *affect* or the noun *effect*), *interface with* (instead of *interact with*), *robust* (instead of *strong*), and *actionable* (instead of *practical*).

As Barzun put it, jargon is often inspired by "a desire to dignify the subject and the writer, coupled with the belief that important matters require a special vocabulary."[4] But jargon can also be less dignified and formal than plain-language substitutes. Consider the trendy business terms *reach out* (for *call, email,* or *contact*),[5] *circle back* (for *revisit*), and *drill down* (for *investigate*).

One insidious form of jargon occurs when useful terms with established meanings are diluted into buzzwords: government health pamphlets are not *literature*, and not every software program uses *artificial intelligence.*

Legalese is a species of jargon peculiar to lawyers. It is characterized by practices such as using the pronoun *said* (instead of *that* or *it*), overusing the verb *shall*,[6] making indirect references such as *the above-captioned case*, and using ritual phrases such as *Comes now before the court.*

Legalese must be distinguished from *terms of art.* The latter are technical terms referring to a legal concept that would otherwise require explanation. Examples of terms of art include *negligence* (which, unlike *carelessness*, is a tort) and *res ipsa loquitur* (a term from negligence law with no plain-language equivalent).

Terms of art are necessary, but purge your writing of legalese. Here are some examples of words and phrases to delete or replace:

- for the foregoing reasons
- herein, hereinafter, therein, thereof, whereof
- in the affirmative, in the negative
- in the instant case

Ritual phrases are an especially obnoxious form of legalese. Some are meaningless incantations whose sole purpose is to communicate that the writer is a member of the bar; others are stuffy substitutes for ordinary language.

Consider these recitals from a poorly written bond contract (with legalese and ritual phrases in bold):

WITNESSETH:

WHEREAS, for its lawful corporate purposes, the Company has **duly authorized** the issue of its 8% Convertible Second Lien Notes due 2013 (**hereinafter** sometimes called the "Notes"), in an aggregate principal amount **not to exceed** One Hundred Fifty Million United States Dollars ($150,000,000), and to provide the **terms and conditions** upon which the Notes are to be **authenticated, issued, and delivered,** the Company has **duly authorized** the **execution and delivery** of this Indenture.

NOW, THEREFORE, THIS INDENTURE **WITNESSETH:**

The archaic *witnesseth* defies both grammar and logic; an indenture cannot "witness" anything.

Litigation documents often include ritual phrases, too. Here's an example from a motion to dismiss:

The Highland Hills Homeowners Association Inc., a Nonprofit Corporation incorporated under the rules and regulations of TITLE 10, Arizona Revised Statutes, comes now before the court requesting that this corporation's Motion to Dismiss this action be received favorably by the court.

This can all be replaced by a much shorter sentence:

The court should dismiss this action.

Other ritual phrases commonly found in legal documents include the following:

Litigation filings

- comes now before the Court
- even assuming, *arguendo*
- further affiant sayeth not
- hereinafter referred to as

- in the above-captioned case
- Plaintiff respectfully requests that . . .
- To all parties and their attorneys of record:

Contracts

- corporation organized and existing under the laws of California
- dated as of even date hereof
- for good and valuable consideration, the receipt of which is hereby acknowledged
- hold harmless
- party of the first part

3.4. Prefer concrete, specific nouns. Minimize vagueness.

Lawyers tend to write in unnecessarily vague ways. This habit taxes readers' brains while making prose harder to read and less informative.

Readers are better at processing and remembering concrete, visualizable words than abstractions. Concrete words also increase clarity because different readers are more likely to have a shared understanding of what the word means. If a city starts a campaign to fix potholes but calls it a "physical safety hazard remediation program," no one will know what the campaign does.

Here are a few example revisions:

- facility → office building
- on or about June 30 → on June 30
- several → six
- vehicle → car

The advice to use fewer abstract words can be taken too far, however, resulting in the vice of overparticularization.[7] All details in your document must be there for a reason—typically because they are legally relevant or add narrative color. Highly specific noun phrases such as *four-door Volvo sedan* contain embedded details. Using such a phrase raises the question of why those details matter. If they don't, the generic *car* may be a better choice.

Vagueness

Words and phrases are vague if they have undefined boundaries. Some vagueness is unavoidable in legal writing because the law involves general rules created to govern unknown real-world scenarios, each of which will likely differ in some way from previous transactions or disputes involving the same rule. Many legal standards and other terms of art are therefore intentionally vague: *commercially reasonable, trade custom, substantial performance, good faith,* and so on.

Rather than using such vague terms freely, use them only when necessary to refer to a legal rule. Words that are terms of art in some contexts, but that are commonly used outside those contexts, include the following—avoid them if you can:

- condition
- duty
- good faith
- reasonable
- right
- substantial

Vague phrases and buzzwords that are *not* terms of art should usually be replaced with more specific descriptions that the reader can visualize. This excerpt from a trade secrets complaint is an example of what to avoid (with vague terms in bold):

> The **information** provided to retailers about shoppers is **overlaid and enhanced** with Plaintiff's **artificial intelligence and predictive analytics**.

Such allegations are conclusory and do not provide enough notice of the facts on which the plaintiff's claims are based.[8] Here's a possible revision:

> The company's software generates purchase predictions and other insights about shoppers.

3.5. Prefer English terms to foreign terms.

For centuries, English-speaking lawyers have ornamented their writing with Latin. Use English instead. For example, consider revising these terms:

- de facto → in practice
- even assuming, arguendo → even if
- *inter alia* → among others
- res judicata → claim preclusion

Note that although the terms below are Latin, they have been assimilated into legal English as terms of art. They may be used and should not be italicized:

- alter ego
- ex parte
- guardian ad litem
- habeas corpus
- in pari delicto
- inter vivos
- pari passu
- ultra vires

You can find definitions of these terms in the notes if any are unfamiliar.[9]

3.6. Minimize hedging.

Lawyers' habitual caution can lead them to write weak prose. If you're thinking about qualifying an assertion with a *hedge* such as one of these words or phrases, consider whether you can drop the hedge and trust that the reader will understand your meaning through the assertion alone:

- could
- for the most part

- likely
- may
- often
- seemingly
- sometimes
- to a certain extent
- usually

If you need to hedge, try constraining the range of possibilities. For example, the frequency indicator *sometimes* is especially vague because it gives readers no sense of how often something occurs. Can you replace it with the more specific *rarely* or *occasionally*?

Style and prudence can conflict on this point. Hedges weaken prose, but attorneys cannot count on all readers being charitable. Avoiding hedges altogether may create an opening for an opponent to paint you as having overstated your case.

Similarly, making unhedged statements to clients about what the law is or how likely a claim is to succeed can be dangerous if there is any reasonable uncertainty about an outcome. The last thing a lawyer wants is to tell a client that their lawsuit is a sure thing and then lose. Anything is possible in a lawsuit, and the judicial process occasionally produces baffling results.

3.7. Use contractions when appropriate.

Contractions are acceptable in formal writing, but many writers are uncomfortable with them because they risk creating a breezy tone—especially if they are overused.

Bryan Garner, an authority on legal writing, endorses contractions and advises writers to aim for "relaxed sincerity."[10] His occasional coauthor, the late Justice Antonin Scalia, disagreed and argued that contractions have no place in formal writing.[11]

Prose stylist Rudolf Flesch suggests the following test: when considering whether to use a contraction, ask "whether you would use the contraction in speaking *that particular sentence*."[12] Someone speaking in a courtroom or other formal setting would probably say *you would* instead of *you'd*.

There are no firm rules governing when to use contractions. The best approach is to train your ear through wide, attentive reading and emulate the writers you admire.

3.8. Avoid clichés.

Resisting clichés is difficult because they are often the first formulations that come to mind when writing. But I am reminded of chess great Emanuel Lasker's advice: "When you see a good move, look for a better one."

Like intensifiers, some common legal clichés risk making the writer sound conclusory or hyperbolic. Consider how you might react upon encountering one of these phrases in an opponent's brief—chances are, the phrase would incline you to disagree with whatever statement it accompanies:

- beyond doubt
- blackletter law
- grievous error
- it goes without saying
- it is crystal-clear

Other phrases are stale and tend to be overused by litigators:

- add insult to injury
- all things considered
- at first blush
- at the end of the day
- back on track

- by the same token
- come full circle
- distinction without a difference
- fall on deaf ears
- foregone conclusion
- in the same vein
- in whole or in part
- misses the mark
- no uncertain terms
- play fast and loose
- time is of the essence

Here are some examples of clichéd language (in bold) from litigation filings and judicial opinions:

California's **landmark case** dealing with the problem of noise from jets taking off and landing at an airport is *Loma Portal Civic Club v. American Airlines, Inc.* [This fact situation is too narrow to have its own "landmark case."]

The argument **misses the mark**.

This case is **on all fours** with *Smith v. Jones*.

The state constitution provided that the questions of compensation and necessity should be passed upon by **one and the same** jury.

We cannot say that the issue is so **open and shut**.

The Court rejected the argument that *Lingle* stood for a **sea change** in the law that precluded the possibility of plaintiffs making facial challenges that could bypass the requirement of being denied just compensation.

The UMWA determined that **sweeping changes** were necessary.

Such phrases are fine for a first draft, but when you revise, challenge yourself to use fresh language. Fresh language is more likely to hold the reader's interest.

3.9. Choose your words precisely.

> Can I say, looking at single words, that every one of them
> means and connotes what I think it does?
> —Jacques Barzun, *Simple & Direct: A Rhetoric for Writers*

Two words can be synonymous without being interchangeable or equally suited to a particular sentence. Every word has its own nuances, connotations, and idiomatic links to other words.

Here are some variables that may affect a writer's choice of words:

Meaning. Words typically have nuanced shades of meaning, and many words are approximate rather than exact synonyms. Rather than thinking of synonyms as equivalents, it may help to think of them as occupying the same neighborhood of meaning. A word's meaning includes its *denotation* (core meaning) and *connotation* (what the word implies besides its core meaning). Consider the approximate synonyms *rough* and *uneven*. Variation in the height of a line may make the line *uneven* without making the line *rough*. *Rough* connotes a state of being unfinished or unpolished, while something can be *uneven* by design (as with *uneven bars*, a gymnastics device).

Vagueness or level of abstraction. Some words encompass broad concepts that can take many physical forms, while other words are specific. Compare, from vague to specific: *vehicle, truck, 18-wheeler*. Note that the word *vehicle* can theoretically encompass both monster trucks and go-karts. In general, use the most specific word available for your purpose, and beware of unwanted vagueness or ambiguity.

Sound and rhythm. English has around forty-four phonemes. A word's sound is determined by its phonemic sounds and its rhythmic pattern of accented and unaccented syllables. Word sounds can also interact with each other to create effects such as *consonance* and *assonance* (repeating consonant and vowel sounds).

Length. All else equal, longer, multisyllabic words are harder to read.

Frequency and difficulty. Readers recognize high-frequency words more quickly than low-frequency words. Compare, in decreasing order of frequency and increasing order of difficulty: *talk, conversation, discourse, colloquy*.

Erudition or stuffiness. Compare the plain-language *help* to the stuffier *assist,* or the modern *request for relief* to the archaic *prayer for relief.*

Level of formality. Compare, in increasing order of formality: *tell a whopper, fib, lie, deceive, misrepresent.*

Connotations. What associations might the word conjure? Compare *commerce* to *intercourse.*

Collocations. *Collocations* are pairs or groups of words that tend to appear near each other—for example, *jury* and *trial, unfair* and *competition,* or *breach* and *contract.*

Usage. Are there any special rules that make certain words more acceptable than others in a given context? For example, nonlawyers often misuse the term *guilty* (which applies to convicted defendants in criminal cases) for *liable* (which applies to defendants in civil cases).

Allusions. Does a word suggest any literary or cultural allusions? Consider the terms *sin* and *blasphemy*, which are associated with religion. They may seem out of place or suggest irony or sarcasm if the writer does not intend a religious meaning.

Associations, including synonyms and antonyms. A word may trigger associations with synonyms, antonyms, or related words. For example, the word *juicy* may activate the ideas of *moist* and *dry.*

Sentiment. Does the word sound "positive," like *warm*, or "negative," like *cold*? Compare *intervention* (positive) and *meddling* (negative). Although some words carry an obvious positive or negative sentiment, others are subtler. Consider the approximate synonyms *coarse* and *rugged. Coarse* has a negative sentiment, as it can be used to describe a rude or unpolished person. *Rugged* has a positive sentiment, as it calls to mind the praiseworthy trait of resilience in the face of hardship.

3.10. Avoid gendered language.

Norms around gender and language are changing. The plural pronouns *they* and *their* are increasingly used to refer to singular antecedents. The masculine pronouns *he* and *his* are no longer considered acceptable stand-ins for persons of unspecified or unknown gender. Words such as *actor* can now encompass people of either gender, and words such as *congressman* are being revised to gender-neutral forms such as *congressperson*. These changes are discussed below.

They *and* their *as singular pronouns*

The most notable recent change in English grammar norms is that the pronouns *they* and *their* are increasingly applied to individuals as well as groups. Traditional grammarians may find that usage jarring, but it is not an error.

Consider the following sentences:

No one knows when *they* will be asked to attend.

No one is singular, and *they* is plural, so this sentence violates traditional grammar rules. The traditional rule would call for *he or she* instead of *they*. But this sentence is grammatically correct.

A good lawyer always communicates with their clients.

A good lawyer is singular, and *their* is plural. But the gender of the abstract good lawyer is indefinite, and there are more options than *he* or *she*, so *their* is at least as acceptable as *his or her*.

Avoid using gendered terms such as *man, men, he, him,* or *his* to stand in for people of all genders. The following sentence will strike many readers as improper in contemporary prose:

A good lawyer always communicates with his clients.

One option when discussing an antecedent with indefinite gender is to pluralize the antecedent, making the plural pronoun *their* available even under traditional rules:

Good lawyers always communicate with their clients.

Another solution is to repeat the antecedent instead of using a pronoun. This can sound clumsy, but it is a good choice in contexts where ambiguity must be avoided. Here is an example (from a contract, with repeated terms in bold):

Either **Attorney** or **Client** may terminate this Agreement earlier upon written notice to the other party; however, if **Client** terminates the Agreement after **Attorney** begins work on the Services, **Attorney** is entitled to full compensation for services performed at the agreed-upon rate and has sole discretion over whether to issue any partial refunds.

Finally, some sentences can be rewritten to avoid the need for a pronoun. Either sentence below is acceptable:

If a student has a question, they should email the professor.

Any student with a question should email the professor.

Avoid strained or unpronounceable pronoun workarounds such as *he/she*, *his/her*, and *s/he*.

Gendered words

Beware of words with built-in gender references. Words like *chairman* and *congressman* have readily available gender-neutral substitutes, while words like *actor* and *waiter* are no longer considered to apply exclusively to men. Here are a few gendered words with suggested revisions:

- actress → actor
- waitress → waiter
- chairman → chair
- freshman → first-year
- weatherman → meteorologist

4 Strong Sentences

The fundamental unit of writing is the sentence. Whether a document is easy to read depends, above all, on whether its sentences are well composed. Readers should be able to understand a sentence in one pass without getting lost and needing to backtrack.

Every sentence in a legal document should provide information that will help or persuade the reader. Many sentences in early drafts will not meet that test and should be deleted. This chapter contains strategies for improving the sentences you decide to keep.

4.1. Keep most sentences short.

Short sentences are easier to read and understand. Long sentences tax readers' patience and working memory. As we read a sentence, working memory allows us to hold the initial words and phrases in mind until we have read enough to analyze the whole sentence.

If a long sentence contains abstract words or unfamiliar terms, as legal sentences often do, it becomes even more demanding on our working memory. The more substantively complex a topic, the shorter and simpler your sentences should be.

Aim for an average length of ten to twenty words per sentence in legal prose. This is a recommended *average*; not every sentence should fall within that range. Prose becomes monotonous if several adjacent sentences have similar lengths and structures.

Just as too many long sentences can put the reader to sleep with rhythmless droning, too many short sentences can sound choppy or staccato. This happens most often in fact sections, where attorneys sometimes sap a story of its vitality by adopting the expressionless style of a police report:

> Before leaving the scene, Baxter took the jewelry Diana was wearing. Baxter then drove off in the Toyota he had stolen earlier that day. Later that night, Baxter showed Diana's jewelry to Castaneda. Baxter gave one of Diana's rings to his then girlfriend, Valentina.

This example contains four sentences of similar length (ranging from nine to thirteen words and seventeen to eighteen syllables), totaling forty-four words. The following suggested revision is more concise and varied, using two sentences of varying length (fourteen words with twenty-three syllables, and nineteen words with thirty-three syllables), totaling thirty-three words:

> Before driving off in the stolen Toyota, Baxter took the jewelry Diana was wearing. Later that night, Baxter showed Diana's jewelry to Castaneda and gave one of Diana's rings to Baxter's girlfriend, Valentina.

All sentences, however long, should be concise. A sentence's length should result from a decision to group information into the sentence, not from a failure to delete unnecessary words.

4.2. Give your prose a sense of forward movement.

Your prose needs a sense of forward movement. As Jacques Barzun explained, "movement makes the difference between prose that reads at a pleasant speed and that which is slow and dull."[1]

Fiction writers discuss the related concept of *pacing*. Successful popular novels, such as those written by John Grisham or George R. R. Martin, are characterized by their rapid pace. If you are drawn into one of their books, you may be able to read hundreds of pages in a day.

Although no court filing is likely to be as engrossing or fast-paced as a popular novel, it's possible to write briefs that leave readers wanting to know more, that motivate them to keep reading.

Consider this good example (from a complaint) and notice how each sentence propels the reader into the next:

> Californians are flocking to on-demand work. Instead of a daily commute, an outdated workplace hierarchy, and the daily grind of an inflexible 9-to-5 job, these workers enjoy the freedom to be their own bosses, set their own hours, and earn income whenever they want. Many such workers also choose to "multi-app" (i.e., simultaneously use the apps of several companies). By using multiple apps at the same time (e.g., Uber, Postmates, Grubhub, and DoorDash), independent service providers can more easily find service requests to perform.

How is this "forward movement" effect achieved? Each sentence is energetic. Each discusses people rather than ideas, and actions rather than states. And each gets right to the point. None is burdened by an introductory windup, such as "Plaintiff wishes to draw the Court's attention to the fact that. . . ." The sentences have rhythm and are divided into digestible segments of sound and meaning.

4.3. Move quickly to the heart of a sentence.

Legal readers want you to get to the point as quickly as possible. Sentences should reveal their substance early, without making the reader wade through contentless introductory text. Avoid *throat-clearing phrases* like these:

- It should be noted that . . .
- It is respectfully requested that . . .
- In this brief, we will argue that . . .

Short words like *and*, *but*, *yet*, and *so* are useful transitions and sentence-starters because they quickly propel readers into the substantive part of the sentence.

Here are two poor examples, with the main clause's subject and verb in bold, followed by suggested revisions. Note in each case how long it takes the reader to find out what action the sentence conveys.

Example 1

Following the passing of Crabtree's mother, but before the generator was fully installed at her residence, **her estate was opened** and Crabtree was appointed to serve as the personal representative.[2]

Suggested revision:

After Crabtree's mother died, Crabtree was appointed to serve as the estate's personal representative. This appointment occurred before the generator was installed.

Example 2

Against this backdrop, it must first be noted that, although Thornton was not provided a Notice to Creditors by the estate's representative (for the reasons described in the Statement of Facts and Section I(c), *infra*, of this Argument Section), **Thornton** nonetheless **petitioned the probate court** to reopen the Estate and, thereafter, was allowed to pursue the underlying action.

Suggested revision:

Although the estate's representative didn't notify Thornton of the debtor's death, Thornton learned of it anyway. Thornton successfully petitioned the probate court to reopen the Estate and was allowed to pursue his claims.

4.4. Write sentences about characters performing actions.

Many sentences in legal writing are static; they lack action and merely describe what exists. Verbs that describe states rather than actions include *is, has, concerns, exists, remains,* and *lacks.* Although such verbs are often unavoidable, try to write about actions rather than states whenever you can.

In lively prose, most sentences feature *characters performing actions.* Stylist Joseph Williams advised writers to introduce a character and action in the first seven words of most sentences.[3]

The "characters performing actions" guideline has two components:

1. **Use an actor as the sentence's subject**. Most sentences' subject should be a person or entity that performs the action of the main verb.

2. **Put the action in the sentence's main verb**. Most sentences should be built around an action verb, not a verb that describes a state. The action should usually be performed by the sentence's subject.

Below are a few examples of how sentences that describe states can be recast as sentences about characters performing actions. One trick: rather than ask *What is the applicable law?*, ask *What must people subject to the law do?*

Example 1

Revisable example (static verb in bold):

Misclassification **is** a misdemeanor under the statute.

Suggested revision (action verb in bold):

The statute **criminalizes** misclassification as a misdemeanor.

Example 2

Poor example (static verb in bold):

Costs such as copying and postage **were** numbers that Johnson simply created without any basis.

Suggested revision (action verb in bold):

> Johnson **charged** clients for made-up copying and postage costs.

Example 3

Poor example (static verb in bold):

> The Fifth District's reasoning **is** wrong in that it shows a misapplication of the "surplusage" rule of contract construction.

Suggested revision (action verb in bold):

> The Fifth District **misapplied** the "surplusage" rule of contract construction.

The next two sections elaborate on the advice that most sentences should use action verbs.

4.5. Use verbs, not nouns, to say what happened.

Writers should usually describe a sentence's action in an action verb, not a noun or prepositional phrase.

Phrases with *buried verbs* (sometimes called *nominalizations* or *zombie nouns*) contain nouns or adjectives that represent the action of a verb. Buried verbs often lurk in nouns ending in *-tion, -sion, -ment, -ity, -ence,* and *-ance*. For example, the noun *enforcement* and its adjectival form *enforceable* encapsulate the action of the verb *enforce*. So too with *utilization* (representing the action *use*), *violation* (representing the action *violate*), and many other words.

Rewrite sentences so that their action is communicated by a verb, as in the following examples.

Example 1

Poor example (phrase containing buried verb in bold):

> The order **is in contravention to** the higher court's three orders.

Suggested revision (action verb in bold):

> The order **contravenes** the higher court's three orders.

Example 2

Poor example (phrase containing buried verb in bold):

> This interrogatory **is violative of** the work-product privilege.

Suggested revision (action verb in bold):

> This interrogatory **violates** the work-product privilege.

Example 3

Poor example (phrase containing buried verb in bold):

> This proposition **is dependent on** defendants' counsel's calculations.

Suggested revision (action verb in bold):

> This proposition **depends on** defendants' counsel's calculations.

Static to be *phrases with buried verbs*

Watch for verb phrases built on the linking verb *to be* (*is*, *are*, etc.). These phrases can often be swapped out for action verbs that convey the same idea. Here are some static phrases and recommended revisions that move the action into a verb:

- is dependent on → depends on
- is in agreement with → agrees with
- is indicative of → indicates
- is lacking in → lacks
- is of the opinion that → believes
- is reflective of → reflects
- is suggestive of → suggests
- it is my intention that → I intend to

Other phrases with buried verbs

The verb phrases below have the same *main verb + buried verb* structure as those above, but their problems are harder to see because they use a main verb other than *is* or *are*. In each problematic phrase, the sentence's action is described in the noun rather than the verb. Each phrase is followed by a suggested revision:

- advance the argument that → argue that
- come to an end → end
- conduct an examination of → examine
- enter into a contract with → contract with
- enter into a settlement agreement → settle
- give approval → approve
- give consideration to → consider
- give permission to → allow
- have the appearance of → appear
- make a contribution → contribute
- make a decision → decide
- make a proposal → propose
- provide a limitation → limit
- reach the conclusion → conclude
- take action → act
- take into consideration → consider

Using dynamic verbs that show action will make your prose more engaging. Instead of the ubiquitous *is* and *has*, try verbs like these:

- dupe
- gaslight
- hoodwink
- purloin
- thwart
- warp

English is rich in verbs; exploit those riches.[4] As an aside, reading a thesaurus is a great way to unwind before bed.

4.6. Write most sentences in active voice.

Active-voice sentences—those in which the sentence's subject performs the action of the main verb—are usually easier to read, more concise, and livelier than passive-voice sentences. Use passive voice only if you have a reason to do so.

First, a quick refresher on how to identify passive voice. In passive-voice constructions, the sentence's subject does not act but is acted on. The actor that performs the action of the main verb is omitted or identified in a prepositional phrase. Here's an example:

Active voice:
The defendant **moved** to dismiss.

Passive voice:
A motion to dismiss **was filed** by the defendant.

Note that both sentences convey the same action, but only the active-voice version describes that action in the sentence's main verb. The active sentence centers on the action verb *moved*, while the passive sentence centers on the linking verb *was*.

While most sentences should be written in active voice, there are many good reasons to use passive voice.

Use passive voice to focus on the object of an action rather than the actor (passive verb and participle in bold):

The claims **were barred** by the statute of limitations.

Use passive voice when the sentence's actor is unimportant, unknown, or up for debate (passive verb and participle in bold):

A war **was started** between the two countries.

Use passive voice if repeatedly using active-voice constructions might create an inappropriate tone. For example, many active-voice sentences starting with "You should" may create a lecturing tone, so this book often uses passive voice (passive verb and participle in bold):

> Most sentences **should be written** in the active voice.

Use passive voice if doing so makes the text more cohesive by creating continuity with the preceding sentence (passive verb and participle in bold):

> In addition to traditional fiduciary duty relationships, such as that of agent and principal, a fiduciary duty exists where there is a "confidential relationship" between two parties. A confidential relationship **can be found** where one party has superior training and knowledge or a dominant position in the relationship.

4.7. Minimize prepositional phrases.

Prepositional phrases can often be revised to make sentences more concise and improve their rhythm, as in the next two examples.

Example 1

Poor example (prepositions in bold):

> Repeat and reiterate each and every denial hereinbefore made **with** the same force and effect **as though** the same were set forth **at** length herein **in** answer **to** paragraph "1142" **of** the Ninety-Fifth Cause of Action **of** the Amended Third-Party Complaint.

Suggested revision:

> Defendant denies Paragraph 1142. Each preceding denial is also incorporated here by reference.

Example 2

Poor example (prepositions in bold):

> Jensen issued notices **under** advice **of** counsel **pursuant to** Section 733.2121, Florida Statutes, **to** what he believed **in** good faith to be the universe **of** creditors **of** his late mother.

Suggested revision:

> Jensen, following his attorney's advice, issued notices under Fla. Stat.
> § 733.2121 to his late mother's creditors.

Note the revision from *creditors of his late mother* to *his late mother's cred-itors*. This illustrates a common revision that can sharpen your writing: consider changing prepositional phrases starting with *of* to possessive noun phrases.[5]

4.8. Keep the subject and verb together near the start of the sentence.

The main components of a sentence are the subject and verb of its main clause. The most readable sentences keep these sentence elements close to each other and reveal them early, as in these examples (subject in bold and main verb in italics):

> **The plaintiff** *moved* to strike the counterclaims.

> **The Court's ruling** *opens* the floodgates for clients who want to shift their losses onto their lawyers.

By contrast, sentences that unduly delay the subject or separate the sub-ject and verb are harder to parse. The sentence below begins with a forty-four-word subordinate clause (main clause's subject and verb in bold):[6]

> Because the buyer had the opportunity to refuse to use Fairmont (as demon-strated by the fact that some buyers elected to use another escrow company and thus Fairmont provided no services, and other buyers objected to the Fairmont fee and obtained a waiver), **Fairmont's use was not** a condition precedent to the purchase.

Suggested revision (main clause's subject and verb in bold):

> The **purchase agreement did not require** buyers to use Fairmont. Some buyers elected to use another escrow company; others objected to Fairmont's fee and had it waived.

Not every sentence should begin with the subject and verb. But the further a sentence strays from the core pattern of keeping the subject and verb next to each other at the beginning of the sentence, the harder it will be for readers to parse. If a sentence is substantively difficult, keep its syntax simple.

4.9. Don't interrupt sentences with citations.

Avoid the common practice of inserting citations in the middle of sentences, interrupting the sentence's flow just to provide bibliographic information that most readers ignore.

Here is a typical example of a sentence weakened by obtrusive midsentence citations:

> A conviction must be reversed where "the record demonstrates a lack of evidence from which a jury could find guilt beyond a reasonable doubt," *United States v. Jimenez*, 705 F.3d 1305, 1308 (11th Cir. 2013), or where "the evidence is so scant that the jury could only speculate or conjecture as to the defendant's guilt," *United States v. Henderson*, 693 F.2d 1028, 1032 (11th Cir. 1982).

Here is a suggested revision of the same text, paraphrasing the rule statements and moving the citations to footnotes:

> A conviction must be reversed where the record shows no evidence from which a jury could find guilt beyond a reasonable doubt,[1] or where the evidence is so minimal that a jury would be forced to speculate about the defendant's guilt.[2]
>
> [1] *See United States v. Jimenez*, 705 F.3d 1305, 1308 (11th Cir. 2013).
> [2] *See United States v. Henderson*, 693 F.2d 1028, 1032 (11th Cir. 1982).

If you don't like footnotes, try to put citations in standalone "citation sentences" rather than allowing them to interrupt ordinary sentences.

4.10. Avoid ambiguous references.

Lawyers often confuse readers by using pronouns with ambiguous referents. If you use a pronoun such as *it, they,* or *that,* be sure the pronoun can reasonably refer to just one antecedent. That antecedent should usually be the noun closest to the pronoun. In this example, the ambiguous pronoun is in bold:

> H&M has not pleaded or proved the extent, if any, to which it will be unable to collect from the Estate as a result of Jensen not providing **it** with notice.

The nearest potential antecedent of the second *it* is "the Estate." But the author is referring to H&M. The ambiguity is resolved by this revision:

> H&M neither pleaded nor proved that it was unable to recover from the Estate because Jensen didn't give notice.

4.11. Keep modifiers near what they modify.

An easy way to make your writing clearer is to place modifiers (including modifying phrases) next to what they modify. Doing so can also help you avoid ambiguity and steer clear of tricky grammatical errors, such as the one in this example:

> Plaintiff's interpretation of Section 5(e) achieves the intent of the statute: to "promote the people's health and safety." By allowing unlicensed school personnel to inject insulin for diabetic students who are unable to do so themselves, such students are able to manage their blood glucose.

The second sentence in this example contains an error: the clause beginning with *By allowing* unintentionally modifies *students*. But the students are not the ones deciding whether to allow unlicensed personnel to inject insulin.

The first sentence also contains two errors of logic. An interpretation cannot act, so it cannot "achieve" an intent (or anything else). And since a statute is not a conscious being, it cannot have an intent. When you revise, check your syntax for logical slips of this sort.[7] Be precise. Here's a suggested revision:

> Plaintiff's interpretation of Section 5(e) achieves the legislature's stated intent of "promot[ing] the health and safety of the people." The statute helps students manage their blood glucose by allowing unlicensed school staff to inject insulin for diabetic students who cannot do so themselves.

4.12. Prefer positive-form statements.

Readers find it easier to think in terms of positives rather than negatives. Double negatives, such as *not unreasonable*, make readers pause to untangle the phrase. Reading legal documents is challenging enough, so don't make the reader do unnecessary mental gymnastics, as in this example:

> It is **not uncommon** for law firms to reorganize and/or attorneys to change firms during the course of a lawsuit.

Suggested revision:

> It is **common** for law firms to reorganize and attorneys to change firms during a lawsuit.

This example borders on self-parody:

> The absence of exceptions was not inadvertent.

Revising *not inadvertent* to *deliberate* would be a good start, but we can do better by rewriting the sentence to describe a character performing an action:

> The legislature deliberately avoided creating exceptions to the rule.

4.13. Use serial commas and hyphenate phrasal adjectives.

Two simple techniques can make your sentences easier to parse.

First, when you write a list of three or more items, always use a *serial comma* before the final item. For example, revise "blue, green or teal" to "blue, green, or teal."[8]

Second, use hyphens to connect *phrasal adjectives* (aka *compound adjectives*) that precede the noun they modify. Phrasal adjectives are multi-word modifiers in which the combined words behave like a single adjective, as with these examples:

- third-party candidate
- single-issue voter
- drive-through restaurant

Using a hyphen to connect these phrases helps the reader correctly group the sentence's words and see that the phrasal adjective should be read as a single modifier. Otherwise, a "third party candidate" might mean the third entrant in a race who belongs to a party, and a "single issue voter" might mean a voter who cares about an issue and is not in a romantic relationship.

4.14. Avoid parallelism errors.

Attorneys often use lists and other parallel structures. These can be rhetorically powerful, and they make writing more organized by giving the reader a mental framework in which to store information.

A claim that the opponent's argument "fails for three reasons" sets up an empty three-shelf bookcase in the reader's mind. The reader will then expect the lawyer to fill those shelves with the promised three reasons— not two reasons and not four—expressed in parallel form. Parallelism failures are broken promises: the writer creates an expectation and then leaves it unfulfilled.

At the sentence level, a parallel structure, such as a list, requires that each of its branches be grammatically parallel and share a common relation to the structure's lead-in phrase. The dog-waste sign pictured in figure 4.1 flunks this test.

Parsing the dog-waste sign
Lead-in phrase: Dog waste is a threat to
    Branch 1: the health of our children,
    Branch 2: our beaches, and
    Branch 3: transmits diseases.

See the problem? *Dog waste is a threat to the health of our children* works, as does *Dog waste is a threat to our beaches*. Branch 1 and Branch 2 are both noun phrases sharing the same relation to the lead-in phrase.

Figure 4.1. A parallelism error
in a park.

But Branch 3, a verb phrase, destroys the parallelism: *Dog waste is a threat to transmits diseases* is nonsensical.

The next example, from a complaint, shows how parallelism errors can drain writing of its persuasive force. The plaintiffs were fashion models who learned that a sex club was marketing itself using their names and likenesses without permission.

> A model's selection of a professional engagement involves a multi-tiered assessment, to wit: (a) determine whether the individual seeking a license of a model's image is reputable, and, through affiliation therewith, would enhance or harm a model's stature or reputation; (b) this reputational information is used in negotiating compensation; (c) to protect her reputation, a model defines the terms and conditions of use; (d) the negotiated deal is memorialized in an integrated agreement.

This sentence, which I've cut in half from the 132-word original, sets up a parallel structure by using a colon before a list. The text before the colon leads the reader to expect a parallel list of the criteria or steps in the model's "multi-tiered assessment," but the writer breaks that promise.

The list's branches are not grammatically or logically parallel. The first branch begins with a verb phrase (*determine whether . . .*), while the other branches begin with noun phrases. Similarly, branches (b), (c), and (d) do not continue the pattern of describing steps in the model's "selection of a professional engagement." It is as though the lawyer forgot what they were writing about midway through the sentence.

You don't need to know all the labels that grammarians assign to clauses and phrases. You just need to notice whether a list's branches share the same grammatical structure. If you read your sentences aloud while revising, your ear should catch such differences.

It's worth considering *rhythmic* parallelism along with grammatical parallelism. The different items in an in-line list should be similar in length. Consider this sentence:

> A model's compensation depends on the work they are hired to do, the time involved, travel, and how their image is going to be used.

Compared with the other listed items, *travel* is rhythmically nonparallel: *travel* has two syllables, while the longest list item, *how their image is going to be used,* has eleven. It is also grammatically nonparallel: *the time involved* has the structure "the [noun] [participle]," so the next item should be something like "the travel required." Suggested revision:

> A model's compensation depends on the work they are hired to do, the time and travel required, and how their image is going to be used.

You can use parallel structures to make long sentences easier to read. The next example is a forty-word sentence that begins with the subject and verb, then follows these core elements with clauses that are grammatically, logically, and rhythmically parallel:

> The Cross-Complaint does not say when this supposed oral lease was agreed to, when rent is due or how it must be paid, who is responsible for taxes and repairs, who must procure insurance, or any other details.

4.15. Use varied sentence structures to control pace and emphasis.

Skilled writers use varying sentence structures to hold the reader's interest, control pace and rhythm, manage transitions, show the relationships among different pieces of information, and allocate emphasis. This section introduces the three main sentence structures in English, which you can learn to use deliberately in your writing: simple, compound, and complex sentences. But first, let's look at a few grammar terms used to explain sentence structure.

A *clause* is a group of words that includes a subject and a verb. An *independent clause* can stand alone as a complete sentence. A *subordinate* (or *dependent*) *clause* cannot stand alone as a complete sentence. It is subordinated to an independent clause, usually using a subordinating conjunction such as *after, although, because, even if,* or *who.* Here's an example:

The plaintiff filed a lawsuit *before the statute of limitations expired.*

The bold text is an independent clause because it can stand alone as a complete sentence. The italicized text is a subordinate clause, linked to the main clause by the subordinating conjunction *before.* With these different types of clauses understood, we can identify the three basic sentence structures.[9]

A *simple sentence* contains one independent clause: "Plaintiff's expert holds an MBA from the University of Chicago."

A *compound sentence* contains two independent clauses separated by a coordinating conjunction (such as *and* or *but*): "Plaintiff's expert holds an MBA from the University of Chicago, and she has held several executive positions at Fortune 500 companies."

A *complex sentence* contains at least one subordinate clause—here, the text before the comma: "Although she has been out of the workforce for seven years, Plaintiff's expert holds an MBA from the University of Chicago and has held several executive positions at Fortune 500 companies."

Let's look at two ways you can use your knowledge of sentence structures to improve your writing.

First, vary the structure of your sentences. Beginning sentence after sentence with the subject or a transition word creates monotony, and placing rhythmically similar sentences back-to-back can create a chanting or sing-song effect. The following well-balanced example shows three adjacent sentences that vary in length, structure, and punctuation:

Aeroflot's unilateral insistence that this case has settled should arouse the Court's suspicions; when parties settle, they agree on that fact and communicate it jointly.

The case has not settled. Aeroflot said that its settlement offer could be accepted only by Plaintiff's return of a signed and notarized release, and Plaintiff refused to sign the release.

Second, use different sentence structures to show the relative importance of information and how different pieces of information relate to each other.

If you want to emphasize information, consider putting it in a stand-alone sentence.

If you want to de-emphasize information, consider putting it in a subordinate clause. Here's an example, with the subordinate clause in italics:

The jury acquitted Crosby on the false-statement counts *while convicting on the fraud counts.*

If two pieces of information are closely related, but one is more important than the other, consider putting them in a complex sentence with the less important information in a subordinate clause. Grouping them in a *compound* sentence instead, with one item in each independent clause, would suggest that the items are equally important.

4.16. Use punctuation to group information within sentences.

Readers process most sentences not as holistic units but as groups of words in which each group plays a grammatical role in the sentence.

Long sentences are easier to read when the reader can immediately perceive how to group the sentence's words into meaningful chunks and how these different chunks relate to each other. This can be facilitated by internal punctuation, but only if the writer knows how to use punctuation correctly. Inexperienced writers tend to both misuse and overuse commas, while avoiding alternatives such as em dashes, colons, semicolons, and parentheses.

Here is a sentence whose commas provide little help to the reader:

> Striking an officer, a violent act, and intoxication, which can result from drug use, do not speak to one's truthfulness.

This example presents a grouping problem. Because parallel groups of three are so common in legal writing, a reader might at first interpret *striking an officer, a violent act, and intoxication* as a parallel list of three items. But the complete sentence shows that the writer intended to create a list of two, not three. *A violent act* is an appositive noun phrase that describes *striking an officer*, while *which can result from drug use* is a relative clause that describes *intoxication*.[10]

One reason the example is difficult to parse is that its commas perform different functions. Two of the commas separate items in a list, while the other two separate the listed items from descriptions of those items. The writer could have eased the reader's path by replacing two of the commas with parentheses and setting the reader's expectations with a *neither . . . nor* framework:

> Neither striking an officer (a violent act) nor intoxication (which can result from drug use) relates to one's truthfulness.

Mid-sentence punctuation allows writers to break sentences into easy-to-read chunks, vary structure and rhythm, and assign emphasis. Here are two good examples. The first shows an effective use of parentheses to land a blow in passing:

> Aeroflot argues (citing no authority) that the Firm's statements of fact in its motion to withdraw are too vague. But any vagueness is inevitable since the allegations are constrained by the attorney-client privilege.

The second uses an em dash to create emphasis and vary sentence structure:

> Franzen failed to produce WhatsApp messages between the parties in the first year of this litigation and suggested in his first deposition that data

from his old phones was unavailable. But in his third deposition, just a month before trial, Franzen admitted that his old phones had been available the whole time—in fact, Franzen keeps them in a desk at his office.

4.17. Monitor your sentences' rhythm.

Rhythmic prose is faster-paced and more pleasant to read. There is no formula for writing rhythmically strong sentences; great writers hone their sense of rhythm over a lifetime of reading.

A key characteristic of rhythmic prose is that it is easier to read aloud. As stylist Richard Lanham put it, good prose contains implicit "performance instructions" to the reader.[11] This concept is best illustrated by children's literature, which often blurs the line between prose and verse:

> And there were three little bears sitting on chairs
> And two little kittens
> And a pair of mittens
>
> —Margaret Wise Brown, *Goodnight Moon*

> "Put me down!" said the fish.
> "This is no fun at all!
> Put me down!" said the fish.
> "I do NOT wish to fall!"
>
> —Dr. Seuss, *The Cat in the Hat*

Ear-pleasing rhythms can also be achieved in legal writing. Consider these closing paragraphs from a motion for sanctions. Note the varying lengths and structures of the excerpt's sentences:

> But Jones did not seek a court order. He decided the matter for himself. He achieved his litigation goals and expelled his partner from the business—not by winning the lawsuit, but by taking the law into his own hands.

Rhythm won't determine whether you win a motion, but it can help you decide how to structure your sentences and paragraphs. If you detect a lack of rhythm in a paragraph, rewrite it.

The subsections below offer strategies for improving your prose's rhythm.

Be concise and use plain language.

In poorly written briefs, rhythmically clumsy or indeterminate sentences are the norm. That is mainly because a lack of rhythm co-occurs with other common flaws in legal writing—unnecessary jargon, overlong sentences, and wordiness. Addressing these problems will tighten your sentences and improve your prose's rhythm.

Think about rhythm in terms of breath units.

Stylist Joe Glaser pointed out that writers can manage rhythm and emphasis by thinking about *breath units* rather than words or sentences.[12] A breath unit consists of the words that come between pauses in a sentence and are spoken in one breath. Each breath unit has a primary stressed syllable, known as *nuclear stress.*

As an exercise, use bars (|) to divide a paragraph you've written into breath units, and then mark the nuclear stresses in each breath unit. In the following examples, notice how each sentence uses punctuation to show the reader where to pause:

> The defendant refused to cooperate in discovery, | so the court imposed sanctions.
>
> However tired I may be, | a grammar lesson wakes me up.
>
> To practice law, | one must develop thick skin.
>
> He's likely to show up late, | if he shows up at all.
>
> The bar exam generally tests substantive knowledge, | not stylistic excellence.
>
> Justice Kennedy, | a Reagan appointee, | wrote the opinion in *United States v. Windsor.*
>
> Learning to write well is, | after all, | a lifelong task.

If you have trouble splitting a sentence into breath units, consider whether the sentence is too long. Watch for uncomfortably long breath units, too—readers shouldn't need voice training to read your prose aloud.

Use punctuation and sentence length to manage rhythm.

Rhythm is mainly determined by sentence-level factors such as punctuation and sentence length. Short sentences tend to be punchy and emphatic, while long sentences can create either a long, rhythmless drone or, if they are well structured, a series of rhythmic cadences.

Punctuation affects rhythm by causing the reader to pause. Different punctuation marks create pauses of different lengths. Here is a list of punctuation marks from shortest to longest pauses:

1. Parentheses
2. A comma
3. A semicolon
4. A colon or em dash (—)
5. Sentence-ending punctuation (a period, question mark, or exclamation mark)

Skilled writers use all these marks to structure their sentences.

Use parallel structures with equally long branches to create rhythm.

Writers and orators often use parallel structures to organize information and create rhythm. One common form is a series of three rhythmically balanced items. You may have heard the memorable phrase coined by a British comedian to describe American GIs in Britain during World War II: "overpaid, oversexed, and over here."

Such rhetorical devices are available to attorneys, too. Consider the following example, from an appellate brief. Note the use of parallelism in the second sentence to create an emphatic cadence:

> The wealth evidence was not an ordinary evidentiary mishap or a fleeting reference to something improper. It was central to the government's case, spanning three days near the end of trial, filling nineteen exhibits, and receiving inappropriate rhetorical emphasis in the government's closing argument.

Parallelism alone does not guarantee that a sentence will be rhythmic. The sentence below has a nearly parallel structure, but its branches are too uneven to create a cadence. The writer gave no thought to rhythm and made no effort to be concise:

> Defendants' conduct is therefore misleading and deceptive by falsely and fraudulently representing that each Plaintiff Model depicted in the misappropriated images is somehow affiliated with Defendants Scarlet Lifestyles LLC or Miami Scarlet Club ("the Club"), has contracted to perform at and/or participate in events at the Club, has been hired to promote, advertise, market, or endorse its swinger or alternative lifestyle events and other activities offered at the Club, has attended or will attend each event, and/or has participated in or intends to participate in the activities advertised.

The items in this sentence are grammatically parallel but not rhythmically parallel, as illustrated in table 4.1. The widely diverging lengths of the parallel structure's branches ruin any rhythm the sentence might have achieved. The biggest problem is the writer's inclusion, in the middle of the sentence, of a thirty-nine-syllable branch that most people cannot vocalize in a single breath.

Table 4.1   Analyzing parallelism in a poorly balanced sentence

Part of parallel structure	Text	Length
Root	Each Plaintiff Model depicted in the misappropriated images	19 syllables
Branch 1	has contracted to perform at and/or participate in events at the Club	20 syllables
Branch 2	has been hired to promote, advertise, market, or endorse its swinger or alternative lifestyle events and other activities offered at the Club	39 syllables
Branch 3	has attended or will attend each event	11 syllables
Final branch	and/or has participated in or intends to participate in the activities advertised.	25 syllables

Consider rhythm when choosing your words.

Rhythm is also affected by word choice. Each word has a pattern of accented and unaccented syllables, and these patterns contribute to a sentence's overall rhythm.

You may remember the patterns below from a high-school poetry lesson. A dash indicates that the syllable is unstressed, a slash that the syllable is stressed.

Metric feet

Two-syllable words
    iamb ($-/$) (Ex: *enough, alert*)
    trochee ($/-$) (Ex: *caution, writing*)
    spondee ($//$) (Ex: *bookmark, sunset*)

Three-syllable words
    anapest ($--/$) (Ex: *understand, comprehend*)
    dactyl ($/--$) (Ex: *poetry, elephant*)

Why should lawyers care? Because if your briefs show a detailed attention to language, including its sounds and rhythms, judges may be more attentive to their contents. They may even enjoy reading them rather than seeing it as a chore.

Read your draft aloud when you edit.

Test your sentences' rhythm by reading your prose aloud as you edit. Read it with feeling, like an actor reading a script, and listen closely to its cadences. Your ear can tell whether a sentence has a discernible rhythm. If you can't easily read a sentence aloud, revise it.

4.18. Monitor your sentences' emphasis.

Because the last word of a sentence echoes briefly in the reader's mind, a sentence's most emphatic position is the end. Good sentences build to a conclusion.

Accordingly, try to end each sentence with a strong word—not, for example, a date, a citation, or a function word like *it* or *that*. As with many style flaws, emphasis problems can often be fixed by tightening the sentence and deleting unnecessary words.

Here are some examples of sentences whose emphasis can be improved:

Mr. Jones passed away yesterday **in Cleveland**.

In this sentence, the reader will momentarily focus on the word *Cleveland* instead of the fact that Mr. Jones died yesterday.

Former plaintiff Kathleen Ryan, Decedent's wife, was deposed **in BC473294 on February 21, 2013**.

It's unlikely that either a case number or deposition date is important enough to mention, let alone emphasize, in a brief's body text. Try not to end sentences with dates or other numbers unless you have a reason to highlight them. Use sentence structure to help the reader focus on your argument rather than on irrelevant details.

A corollary principle is if you want to de-emphasize information, bury it in the middle of your sentences. Defense attorneys often need to bury the bad news about their clients' conduct. In this example from an appellate brief, the attorney de-emphasizes the fact that a jury convicted her client of two crimes (de-emphasized fact in bold):

The jury acquitted Humbert on six of the nine charges against him, failed to reach a verdict on one, and **convicted on only two**, after deliberations spread over twenty-six days.

Consider where the emphasis falls in your sentences and keep in mind that the last word in a sentence is particularly emphatic because it briefly rings in the reader's ear after the sentence concludes. While editing, as you read each sentence aloud, exaggerate the last word. Is that where you want the emphasis to fall? Is that the word you want reverberating in the reader's mind?

Finally, note that writers can manipulate emphasis through mid-sentence punctuation. Em dashes and colons emphasize the text that precedes and follows them by causing the reader to pause and form an expectation about how the sentence will end.

5 Organization and Cohesion

5.1. Use chunking, grouping, and labeling to organize your document.

5.2. Break documents into self-contained modules.

5.3. Use transitions to make documents cohesive.

5.4. Begin with your conclusion.

5.5. Use full-sentence point headings.

5.6. Write unified paragraphs, each centered on one main idea.

5.7. Build paragraphs around topic sentences.

5.8. Use umbrella text to introduce subsections.

This chapter discusses ways to tie text together at the paragraph, section, and document levels. These strategies will help your prose achieve three overlapping writing aims: organization, cohesion, and unity.

An *organized* text is analogous to an organized closet: its audience can easily find what they are looking for, and nothing seems jumbled or out of place. The information you put in lists and outlines should align with what readers expect from such structures. For example, items in a list should be conceptually parallel, with each belonging alongside the others. In an outline, the hierarchy of headings and subheadings should accurately reflect how different parts of the text relate to each other.

Cohesion refers to how different parts of a document hang together through ties such as transition phrases and the repetition of concepts. It distinguishes a document from a collection of sentences. In a cohesive text, no movement between adjacent sentences or paragraphs feels jarring.

Unity refers to the integrity of portions of the text such as paragraphs and sections. A paragraph is unified if each of its sentences pertains to a shared theme or idea.

Organization, cohesion, and unity are essential to written communication.

5.1. Use chunking, grouping, and labeling to organize your document.

Chunking and *grouping*—the act of breaking up wholes into parts or collecting parts into wholes—are central to writing readable documents and making digestible arguments. I use the terms to describe strategies writers can use to ease their readers' cognitive burdens by creatively splitting and grouping information.

As explained in section 1.4, readers have limited cognitive resources for working memory, perception, and attention. At any moment, humans can hold only a few discrete items in their short-term memory.[1]

Writers can use chunking and grouping to simplify a text's demands on the reader by creating an optimal number of ideas or concepts for the reader to think about at one time. Because of the limits on readers' working memory, it's inadvisable to ask readers to remember or think about more than a few pieces of information at once.

After you've decided how to divide information into groups, you can use the strategy of *labeling* to assign a name to each group, making it easier to refer to and reason about.

My favorite examples of grouping in legal briefs occur when an attorney strategically groups issues to simplify the problem facing the court. This invites the court to decide several issues at once in the client's favor.[2]

A good example, reproduced below, appeared in an appellate brief filed by a criminal defense attorney whose client was convicted of fifteen felony counts, each creating independent grounds for a multiyear jail sentence. It was imperative for this attorney to vacate as many of these convictions as possible, but no judge wants to think through fifteen counts. If left to their own devices, the reader will probably group the counts themselves according to an organizational principle that may not align with the appellant's analysis and theme. Alternatively, they might carefully evaluate one or two counts and use these as proxies (heuristics) for the others.

So why not preemptively group the counts by classifying them? In the following example, watch how the attorney deftly switches from discussing fifteen counts to two groups of counts, giving each group a memorable name (in italics):

The fifteen counts fall into two main categories: *the securities counts*, which encompass Count Two (securities fraud) and Counts Three through Five and Seven through Ten (false filings); and *the lying-to-auditors counts*, which encompass Counts Thirteen through Nineteen.

This practice of grouping information is rarely neutral. With the example above, the prosecutor opposing the appeal would likely argue that the "lying-to-auditors counts" cannot be lumped together as a group. Rather, the government would argue, each charged crime of which the defendant was convicted must be analyzed separately, just as the jury had to consider each separately.

Strategically grouping discrete ideas is most persuasive when the classification is unassailable. The logical principle is that all the items in one cluster must be more similar to each other in relevant respects than they are to any items in another cluster.

5.2. Break documents into self-contained modules.

Modularity is a term used by computer programmers to describe the standard practice of writing programs not as one giant script, but as separate, self-contained components that are linked together. For example, a program that provides an operating system for a mobile phone would not store all its code in one file; it would have many separate files for different features, such as wireless connectivity and location services. That way, if something goes wrong with one of these features, that feature can be disabled or restarted without crashing the phone.

The practice of breaking up software code into self-contained and self-explanatory modules makes it much easier to read. Programmers can more easily find what they are looking for and see how a particular block of code fits into the overall program.

Similar reasoning helps explain why attorneys divide briefs into sections, subsections, and paragraphs. Doing so makes text easier to read, in part because smaller blocks of text are more digestible and less visually intimidating.

But while the length of a text block may make us feel the need to create new subsections or paragraphs, where should the text be split? A hint of the answer can be found in programmers' concept of modularity. Each module usually performs a discrete, standalone function—it "does one thing well," to use a tech-industry phrase. The sections and subsections of your briefs should likewise do one thing well.

Every section and subsection needs a definite purpose. For example, a section of a motion to dismiss might explain why the plaintiff has failed to adequately allege an element of a claim in the complaint. That purpose should be accomplished within that section, and the reader should not find arguments on the point scattered throughout the brief. Similarly, every sentence and paragraph in the section should further the section's goal, making the section unified.

5.3. Use transitions to make documents cohesive.

Think about adjacent sentences and paragraphs as links in a chain, with each link pointing backward to previous information. The mechanisms by which a writer creates these backward pointers are called *transitions*.[3]

Transitions are critical to good prose because they promote cohesion and assure readers that they have not lost their place in the document. Without transitions, a piece of writing may feel like it is bouncing around among unrelated topics.

Novice writers are sometimes taught to begin most sentences and paragraphs with a transition term such as *however* or *therefore*. These terms leave no doubt about how a sentence or paragraph relates to the preceding information. But they are just one way to link new information to information communicated earlier. Any of these methods can be thought of as transitions:

Transition terms, such as *further, additionally,* and *but*

Pointing phrases that refer to previous material, such as *Those arguments . . .*

Signposts indicating a reader's position in the argument, such as *First, Second,* and *Third*

Echo links that repeat or allude to a recently mentioned word or concept

Transition terms

Transition terms are an essential ingredient of cohesive writing. Some have the virtue of being short, which increases the writing's readability and pace. These include *also, and, but, here, nor,* and *so.*

Other common transition terms include *accordingly, as a result, however, in short, similarly,* and *therefore.*[4]

Shorter transition terms are preferable to their longer counterparts. *But* is usually better than *however,* and *so* is usually better than *therefore.* But vary your word choice to avoid repetition and to manage rhythm and emphasis.

In this good example, from an answer, note the transition terms (in bold):

> The allegations in Paragraph 42 of the Complaint are alleged solely against the ECF Defendants. **Additionally**, the allegations that "[e]lectrical infrastructure is inherently dangerous" and "[t]he transmission and distribution of electricity requires the ECF Defendants to exercise an increased level of care" are legal conclusions, **so** Boeing need not respond. To the extent a response is required, Boeing lacks sufficient information to admit or deny the allegations, **and** on that basis denies them.

If you use a transition term, make sure the term accurately reflects the relationship between the adjacent sentences or paragraphs. For example, writers sometimes start a sentence with "Therefore," then fail to draw a conclusion derived from the previous sentences. Here's a poor example (inaccurate transition term in bold):

> The defense argues that the crime resulted from computer error, but this incident shows intent or absence of mistake. **Therefore**, the incident is sufficiently like identity theft.

Pointing phrases

Pointing phrases typically use a demonstrative adjective (*this, that, those,* etc.) to refer to a concept already introduced. Here's a good example (pointing phrase in bold):

> The "buy-out fee" is indistinguishable, except in outrageousness of amount, from the early termination fees held to be penalties in *AT&T v. Pearson.*

In that case, the Court of Appeal held that early termination fees of $150 and $200 were unlawful penalties under Cal. Civ. Code § 1671(d).

Here's a good example (pointing phrases in bold) that shows how you can use a pointing phrase to link paragraphs:

> When a network licenses a program, it agrees to pay the producer a per-episode fee. The amount of **that fee** typically depends on the kind of show. In "scripted" television—comedies and dramas—the fee is usually between 50% and 70% of what it costs the producer to make each episode. The cost of producing "unscripted" programs, including game shows, is typically lower, and fees for **such programs** generally equal the producer's costs.
>
> **This structure** means that producers do not make a profit on network license fees alone. Unscripted programs merely break even, and scripted programs lose money.

The phrase *This structure* distills the information in the first paragraph into a single concept. This compression helps the reader's working memory and allows the earlier paragraph to be referred to as a unit.

Signposts

A roadmap tells the reader where they are going, and a signpost tells the reader where they are now. Sentences setting up list frameworks are a common type of roadmap. In legal briefs, paragraphs sometimes begin with a legal proposition, such as "Defendant's argument fails for three reasons." That sentence sets up a structure analogous to a three-shelf bookcase, and the remaining sentences fill that structure with information.

Signposts, such as *First,* act as transitions because they instruct the reader about how the text that follows relates to what the reader read before.

Echo links

Echo links repeat or refer to ("echo") a word or concept that was introduced earlier. I use the term to encompass both verbal and conceptual links.

The simplest way to create an echo link is to repeat a term or phrase from the previous sentence, as in this example (echo links in bold):

> Apartment managers cannot try to enforce a lease and then hide behind the landlord, an undisclosed principal, when the tenant challenges the lease. **Tenants** need not go sleuthing to trace the identity of remote **landlords** through a maze of shell companies such as those used by Homeview's owners.

There are also more oblique references in that paragraph that could be considered echo links. The terms *sleuthing, trace,* and *maze* echo the words *hide* and *undisclosed* by carrying forward their theme. These word choices conjure an atmosphere of secrecy and deception.

Echo links can make cohesion seem effortless and eliminate the need for explicit transitions. In this example, observe how each phrase in bold echoes a word or concept mentioned in the previous sentence:

> Californians are flocking to on-demand work. Instead of a daily commute, an outdated workplace hierarchy, and the daily grind of an inflexible 9-to-5 job, **these workers** enjoy the freedom to be their own bosses, set their own hours, and earn income whenever they want. Many **such workers** also choose to "multi-app"—that is, simultaneously use the apps of several app-based network companies. By using **multiple apps** at the same time—e.g., Uber, Postmates, Grubhub, and DoorDash—**independent service providers** can more easily find service requests to perform.

In short, there are many ways to ensure that your document is cohesive and flows smoothly from one sentence and paragraph to the next. As you revise, if you find a section that feels disjointed, consider whether you can use one of these transition devices to link your sentences and paragraphs.

5.4. Begin with your conclusion.

Legal documents are not detective stories. Judges and clients want immediate answers, followed by reasons supporting those answers. It's best to assume that whoever reads your brief will skim it rather than reading it from start to finish, and the first thing they will look for is a conclusion.

In legal briefs, the overall conclusion is typically a contention that the court should grant or deny legal relief. That conclusion, together with the main arguments supporting it, forms the skeleton of your document. Therefore, begin the document with its conclusion and each section with the section's conclusion.

The following paragraph from a brief appropriately puts the conclusion in a point heading before stating and applying a rule that leads to the conclusion:

> **The petitions for review should be dismissed for lack of jurisdiction.**
>
> Under the Clean Air Act, a party may obtain judicial review of an EPA rule after the initial 60-day review period ends only if its petition is "based solely on grounds arising after such sixtieth day" and is "filed within sixty days after such grounds arise." 42 U.S.C. § 7607(b)(1). These requirements are jurisdictional, and Petitioners flouted them. They did not seek judicial review within 60 days of the point-of-obligation rule's promulgation in 2010.

In legal briefs, the principle that attorneys should build their documents around the conclusion has an important corollary: avoid building around the *opponent's* conclusion or blindly following the structure laid out in the opposition's brief. Play offense, not defense.

Rather than responding point-by-point to the other side's argument, make your own affirmative argument, explaining the law as you see it. Respond to counterarguments only after making your affirmative argument under each point heading.

5.5. Use full-sentence point headings.

Headings create the framework for a legal document and allow readers to understand your arguments at a glance.

When you outline a brief, create placeholder headings that track the logic of your arguments and show how they interrelate. Then, as you draft, the point headings can serve as focal points for all the information you put within each section, ensuring that the sections are unified. Each paragraph beneath a point heading should relate to the point heading and provide a reason the heading is correct.

Once you're satisfied with the document's structure, turn your point headings from placeholders into tools for persuading the reader while making your argument structure clear. Strong point headings make your reasoning easy to track and your briefs easy to skim. If your point headings are informative and persuasive, a judge should be able to understand the gist of your arguments just by reading the table of contents.

Because point headings are more likely to be carefully read than any other part of a brief, they are a key opportunity to communicate with the court. Many attorneys squander that opportunity. Here are some examples of poor headings found in legal briefs—note how each fails to inform or persuade:

Trial Court Erred in Sustaining a Demurrer Without Leave to Amend.

ISSUE 5: Whether a genuine issue of material fact on Appellant's contract claim precluded the grant of summary judgment.

THE INVALIDITY JUDGMENT SHOULD BE REVERSED.

DUPONT'S INTERNAL DOCUMENTS

The Broad Application of Section 190.3, Factor (a), Violated Appellants' Constitutional Rights.

DEFENDANT FAILS TO SATISFY THE RULE 12(b)(6) STANDARD.

A good default formula for first- and second-level point headings in briefs is "[Conclusion] because [Reason]." In other words, an ideal point heading states the proposition you want the judge to adopt after reading the section, then previews your best argument for the proposition.

Here are some good examples of point headings that further a brief's arguments while telling the reader what to expect within each section:

Charges imposed only upon breach are not "options for alternative performance" because breach is not performance.

The cases Equity discusses—none of which involve an adhesion contract—are irrelevant.

The district court erred in certifying the settlement class because Rule 23(a)(4)'s adequacy requirements were not satisfied; the zero-recovery subclass required separate representation.

The securities convictions should be reversed because the prosecution failed to offer sufficient evidence of a material GAAP violation.

The FDA violated its own regulations that interpret the three-year exclusivity provisions.

TransCorp did not prove that plasma-fluorinated polymeric material was in public use before the critical date.

5.6. Write unified paragraphs, each centered on one main idea.

According to one stylist, paragraphing "is largely a visual contrivance," so the optimal length of a paragraph "depends on how it strikes the eye."[5] But writers should not arbitrarily create paragraph breaks, as in this poor example:

Now that Juniper has Alteria's infrastructure, progress in nicotine cessation stands to erode. Defendants use the very fraudulent and deceptive youth marketing business practices adjudged to violate federal racketeering laws.

They exploit themes that resonate with teenagers while falsely denying doing so: Plaintiff brings this lawsuit to redress the harm already sustained and to prevent future harm to others.

There is no reason for starting a new paragraph after "laws." What should be a single paragraph has been arbitrarily broken in two.

The most common reason for starting a new paragraph is that you intend to make a new point or discuss a new idea. Each paragraph develops a single idea that furthers the current section's argument or narrative. When you start a new paragraph, you show the reader that they are moving from one idea to the next.

In most well-structured legal writing, you can glance at a paragraph and see what function it is playing in the document's argument.

5.7. Build paragraphs around topic sentences.

At the beginning of a paragraph, use one of the transition devices discussed in section 5.3 to show how the paragraph connects with its predecessor. Then provide a *topic sentence* showing what the paragraph will discuss. The topic sentence creates a focal point for the paragraph's remaining sentences, each of which should add information that relates to the paragraph's main idea.

Many topic sentences state propositions that are supported or explained by the rest of the paragraph. For example, a paragraph might begin with the following topic sentence:

> The Cross-Complaint admits that Russell did not rely on Schmidt's alleged misrepresentations in making the loans.

The rest of the paragraph would support that proposition by quoting the cross-complaint's admissions and explaining their significance. Anything unrelated to the admissions or the issue of reliance should be put in a different paragraph.

Topic sentences are more effective if they use your own words and are not interrupted with citations. Here's a good example of a paragraph that begins with a proposition, then backs it up with reasoning supported by a citation:

> The contract provision at issue is not a liquidated damages clause, so the bankruptcy court erred in evaluating it under that legal framework. Because the clause operated only prospectively to an amount concededly owed, the amount charged was interest, not a penalty. *See Thompson v. Gorner,* 104 Cal. 168, 170 (1894).

5.8. Use umbrella text to introduce subsections.

After a heading but before any subheadings, include "umbrella text" that introduces the subsections that follow. This paragraph can link the section to the brief's overall theme, provide a high-level summary of the section's arguments, or show the reader a roadmap for the section's subheadings.

Here's a good example of umbrella text (between the headings) that expands on the point heading and tells the reader what to expect from the subsections that follow:

> **III. The prosecution failed to offer sufficient evidence of mens rea on any count.**
>
> Each count required the prosecution to prove beyond a reasonable doubt that Mr. Goyal had actual knowledge that statements in NAI's financials or management letters were false when made. The evidence fell far short.
>
> **A. Every count required proof of actual knowledge that a statement was false when made.**

You can also use umbrella text to provide rule statements or other information that applies to all subsections below the main point heading. This organizational trick is analogous to factoring in math: you pull out information that is common to each subsection and handle it in one place rather than having to revisit it several times.

Here's an example (umbrella text between the headings):

> **II. The preliminary injunction standard is met. Barger's opposition filings show that he has no defense to Mapp's claims and will not be harmed by an injunction.**
>
> In deciding whether to issue a preliminary injunction, courts consider two interrelated factors: the likelihood the moving party ultimately will prevail on the merits, and the relative interim harm to the parties from the issuance or nonissuance of the injunction. Both factors favor Mapp.
>
> **A. Barger's new admissions make it even more clear that Mapp will prevail on his claims.**

6 Tone and Professionalism

6.1. Advocate ethically.
6.2. Write in a professional tone.
6.3. Don't disparage opponents.
6.4. Don't try to be humorous or literary.
6.5. Write respectfully about judges.

There is more to persuasion than making sound arguments and citing apt authority. The work you put into your legal documents can be undermined by ethical breaches (real or perceived), lapses into unprofessionalism, or the use of an inappropriate tone. This chapter provides a few guidelines on these points.

6.1. Advocate ethically.

Integrity and professionalism are paramount in legal practice. They must override your competitive drive, desire to help a client, concerns about finances and status, and all other considerations. Treat them as strict constraints on your advocacy.

These values can be guides as well as constraints, however. Ethical rules limit what arguments you can make, but in so doing, they help you focus on arguments that are relevant and persuasive.

Attorneys may not mislead courts by presenting assertions they know to be false as true, helping their clients commit perjury, or advocating frivolous legal positions. Rule 11 of the Federal Rules of Civil Procedure and parallel rules in state statutes bar attorneys from bringing frivolous claims and advocating frivolous positions—claims and positions that any reasonable attorney would know to be baseless. These ethical rules also require attorneys to sign their filings and, through their signature, represent to the court that the filing is not being presented for an improper purpose; that its legal arguments are warranted; and that its assertions and denials of fact have (or are reasonably believed to have) evidentiary support.[1]

Some attorneys try to gain an advantage through unfair or unethical litigation tactics such as these:

Attempting to mislead the court about a statement made, action taken, or position argued by the opponent. Attorneys often misrepresent what the opposing party said or did by taking quotations out of context, inaccurately summarizing or paraphrasing a statement, omitting parts of a correspondence chain, or unfairly describing an opponent's position.

Attempting to mislead the court about the law. Attorneys sometimes argue that the relevant legal rule is supplied by an out-of-context quotation from an irrelevant case, fail to distinguish holdings from dicta in the cases they cite, rely on unpublished or superseded judicial opinions without noting these infirmities, or otherwise attempt to mislead the court about the relevant law.

Relying on testimony the attorney knows to be false. Just because some clients may be willing to perjure themselves does not mean you can knowingly help them do so. If you know that a client is withholding documents responsive to a discovery request, for example, you should not file and rely on that client's sworn declaration (affidavit) claiming to have produced all documents.

Mischaracterizing procedural history. Judges are so busy that they may need to be reminded about how they ruled on earlier motions. Attorneys sometimes try to capitalize on this by inflating favorable rulings and claiming that the court ruled on issues it did not reach.

Attorneys who use such tactics violate the rules of fair competition and professional ethics. If caught, they risk permanently losing credibility with the judge or other members of the bar.

Rather than cross the line into dirty tricks, make a nonnegotiable commitment to argue fairly. I think of it this way: your legal briefs and arguments should help judges reach correct decisions that further your clients' interests. Your aim is not to fool or confuse judges into making incorrect decisions.

What if you can't imagine any correct decision in which your client would prevail? Settle the case or withdraw as counsel. The next time a prospective client knocks on your door, ensure that you can see a path toward helping them achieve their goals while staying within the boundaries of the law and professional ethics. If the prospective client wants you to file a claim that you suspect may lack legal or factual support, do your research before accepting the case.

6.2. Write in a professional tone.

> You should pretend you're talking to a person across a table
> in a quiet room. . . . The best briefs are models of simple
> clarity and restraint.
> —Steven D. Stark, *Writing to Win: The Legal Writer*

Tone is a matter of professionalism as well as style. By consistently using an appropriate tone, you avoid annoying the reader while doing your part to uphold the dignity of the legal profession.

Write in a reasonable tone and show that you are trying to help the judge correctly decide the issue by explaining the relevant facts and law. Focus on making the strongest affirmative argument for your client's position. Doing so will help you avoid focusing on the opponent and being reactive or defensive.

The most important tone guidelines for litigators are these:

- Ensure that your prose is understated, not overwrought, pompous, or laden with overt emotional appeals.
- Write to persuade the reader, not to harass or disparage your opponents.
- Always show respect to judges.

Here are some mistakes to avoid:

- Using slang or other overly casual language
- Using humor or folksy expressions
- Attempting to be "literary"

- Using hyperbole
- Sounding strident (e.g., overusing intensifiers such as *flagrantly*)
- Overstating your points (e.g., saying that a fact "proves" a conclusion when it merely provides evidence supporting that conclusion)

The remaining sections in this chapter elaborate on and provide examples of these points.

6.3. Don't disparage opponents.

Judges can't stand sniping between counsel, so resist the temptation to engage in it. Don't take the bait. This is often easier said than done. For example, an opposing attorney once sent an email advising me to stop "whining" because it was "unbecoming." File such emails away in case you need them later, but don't respond.

Litigation should focus on the parties and their claims, not the attorneys and their personalities. Refrain from personal attacks against the opposing party or counsel. Such attacks have little or no persuasive value and may even elicit sympathy for the opponent. When possible, avoid mentioning opposing counsel entirely and simply discuss the law and facts.

Here are some examples of what to avoid, all from a single filing:

Although Plaintiff is technically pro se, he is a sophisticated attorney who either could not be bothered to research the procedural requirements of his own motion, or blatantly chose to disregard them.

Plaintiff's assurances were clearly disingenuous, as his next move was to file this instant motion without the safe harbor period or any effort to meet and confer, directly contradicting his own position.

Indeed, Plaintiff's modus operandi in this case has been to engage in rhetoric that is nothing more than a consistent effort to bully and intimidate the defense through never-ending, frivolous threats of sanctions.

Because of the procedural defects and substantive misrepresentations in this motion, Defendants can only conclude that Plaintiff, as is his course of practice, brings this motion in bad faith for the purpose of causing the parties, and this Court, to waste its resources and efforts defending against yet another senseless motion.

That brief's author intended to inspire the judge with righteous anger but instead came across as petty. Don't make the same mistake.

6.4. Don't try to be humorous or literary.

A filing is never about the lawyer who wrote it; it's about the law, the client, and the story you are trying to tell. Attempts to be funny or "literary" distract the reader and shift their focus from the point you are trying to make.

Attempts at humor tend to fall flat in legal settings because people's rights and livelihoods are on the line. Attempts to be literary (through allusions, flowery language, or poetic detail, for example) spotlight the writer rather than the client and the law.

Here are two examples of attempts to be humorous or literary that predictably fall flat. The first is an ill-conceived biblical allusion:

> The Hortons contend that the policy should exempt them from liability as good Samaritans. To the contrary, the Hortons were not the good Samaritans; they were the "thieves" as far as continuing with the parable.[2]

The second is a passage in which whatever point the attorney is trying to make disappears in a cringeworthy fusion of folksy language and literary cliché:

> It is unsurprising that the very same defendants that videoed plaintiff John Smith while he was on vacation and after he was terminated would object to his counsel's use of the words "criminal," "illegal," "tailing," and "invasion of privacy" at trial. Perhaps we live in a more Orwellian society than old George predicted.

Such devices serve no purpose and are likely to annoy a judge.

6.5. Write respectfully about judges.

Rules of legal ethics require advocates to uphold the "dignity of the tribunal" and behave as "officers of the court." Judges are put off by any show of disrespect to themselves or their colleagues, so address and refer to them deferentially, even when you believe they are wrong.

A common mistake is to make assertions about what a judge "must" do. However little discretion a judge may have in applying a rule, there is usually some escape hatch they can use to justify a decision. And even if it's true that the judge must do something, a litigant should never say so. You are better off having the judge reach that conclusion on their own after reading your brief.

The opposite mistake of excessive deference (even obsequiousness or flattery) should also be avoided. This mistake most commonly occurs through attorneys' use of formulaic introductory phrases, such as "Plaintiff respectfully requests that . . ."

The one-syllable verb *should* is the optimal middle ground between these extremes:

> The Court must reverse . . . → The Court should reverse . . .

> Plaintiff respectfully requests that the District Court's ruling be affirmed in each and every respect. → The Court should affirm . . .

One application of this principle arises if you are appealing a lower court's ruling. However frustrated you may be with the court's mistake, refer to the court respectfully.

Appellants have an uphill battle because they must persuade judges to reverse a colleague, which can seem like a public rebuke of the lower-court judge. Therefore, appellate lawyers should raise their points "more in sorrow than in anger."[3] Diatribes like these are unacceptable:

> **The district court failed even to address** several aspects of the mental-health system that Defendants demonstrated are constitutional—screening, records and medication management, and protocols for use of force and discipline concerning mentally ill inmates. **In the court's mistaken view,** because the State had "gone for the home run ball" by seeking to terminate the whole case, it was not entitled to have the court consider the appropriateness of its control over individual aspects of the mental-health system.

Err on the side of professionalism and use a neutral tone when describing a judge's actions.

PART II   Substance

7 Briefs and Motions

Most litigated motions have plausible arguments on both sides, giving judges discretion to decide the motion either way. This is where a litigation attorney's writing skills can be decisive. Attorneys can design strong arguments backed by thorough research, then communicate those arguments persuasively.

Writing style and argumentation are intertwined; a poorly written brief often reflects a poorly conceived argument, and even a strong argument can succeed only if the judge understands it and is moved to accept it. In the end, though, substance is more important than style in legal writing. A beautifully written brief cannot salvage an untenable argument.

In this chapter and the next two, we consider the substantive side of litigation writing: how to design persuasive arguments and tell your client's story.

7.1. Assert propositions, then support them.

A *proposition* is a statement that can be accepted or rejected. For example, "employers are liable for the negligence of their employees if the employees were acting within the scope of their employment" is a proposition of law; "the driver was making a delivery for the defendant at the time of the accident" is a proposition of fact.

Legal arguments combine propositions of law and fact to show that the preferred conclusion is more probable than not. Propositions are therefore the building blocks of legal argument.

If you disagree with the conclusion asserted by your opponent, the most common way to attack that conclusion is by challenging its underlying premises—that is, the statements of law and fact that purportedly lead to the conclusion. Correspondingly, to be able to anticipate and defeat counterarguments, you must be alert to how your premises could be challenged and prepare to back them up with citations to authority and other devices.

Law students often learn to think about legal arguments in terms of cases rather than propositions. But the main reason to cite a case is to provide backing for a proposition. Your argument should be built around propositions, not cases that support those propositions.

It follows that most paragraphs in your argument section should begin with propositions followed by supporting authority. Use the pattern of *proposition + backing* rather than the more common *backing + proposition*. This is another way to state the advice that legal writers should lead with and organize around their conclusions.

Thinking in terms of propositions will help you better understand the structure of your arguments. This in turn will help you make that structure clear to the reader. You'll also begin to catch yourself whenever you start to digress and write something in your brief's argument section that doesn't advance any of the propositions needed to make your case.

I suggest this approach:

1. Divide your argument into propositions: the conclusions and sub-conclusions you must establish to convince the judge of your overall conclusion.

2. Organize these propositions in a logical way to help yourself and, ultimately, the reader follow the argument's reasoning. Note whether any of the propositions are mutually dependent or mutually exclusive.

3. Determine whether each proposition is likely to be contested and whether strong arguments exist against it. Uncontested or self-evident propositions need not be explained, and some can be implied

rather than spelled out. The more debatable a proposition is,
however, the more you will need to support it.

Unless you have good reason to do otherwise, begin each paragraph in
your brief's argument section with a proposition that will serve as one of
the steps toward your conclusion. Cases support propositions, but they are
not themselves propositions. Don't leave the reader to infer what propositions the brief is trying to establish.

The excerpt below is a poor example from a summary judgment brief
that illustrates several related mistakes. It begins discussing a case without saying why the case matters or what proposition it supports. It then
launches into details without providing context, and uses a block quotation (whose relevance is unclear) to substitute for analysis:

B. The Facts in This Case Permit an Inference of Common Reliance on the False Representations and Concealments of Nokia

In *Massachusetts Mut. Life Ins. Co. v. Superior Court*, the plaintiff brought a
class action against an insurance company under the CLRA and the UCL
concerning the practices of the insurance company in selling "vanishing pre-
mium" policies. The plaintiff alleged that the defendant misrepresented the
amount of dividends it would pay over time. The court stated at pp. 78–79:

> Causation as to each class member is commonly proved more likely than not
> by materiality. That showing will undoubtedly be conclusive as to most of
> the class. The fact a defendant may be able to defeat the showing of causa-
> tion as to a few individual class members does not transform the common
> question into a multitude of individual ones; plaintiffs satisfy their burden
> of showing causation as to each by showing materiality as to all.

In the case at bar, the Nokia Defendants failed to disclose the cumulative effect
of their standard billing practices on the number of actual airtime/talk time
minutes contained in each and every Nokia rate plan. [citations omitted]

The attorney should have located the reader within the argument (think
of a "you are here" dot on a map), stated the proposition for which the case
provides support, and only then discussed the case. When discussing it,
the attorney should have begun by stating a bottom-line point showing
the reader why they should care about the case. The discussion should
have been kept as short as possible, with the relevant analysis supplied
mainly in the attorney's own words.

The next example contains useful raw materials for an argument, but the writer should extract and lead with the relevant propositions:

> The court further stated in *Anunziato* at page 1138: "Where the manufacturer of a product makes a false representation as to weight or count . . . the consumer is unquestionably harmed as a result of the falsity because he was short-changed." That is exactly the situation in the case at bar. Nokia made a misrepresentation to all of its subscribers as to the number of usable airtime minutes in each of its service plans/rate plans, and as a consequence, each and every Nokia subscriber was short-changed on airtime minutes.

This excerpt begins with the proposition that a court made a certain statement in a case called *Anunziato*. But how does *Anunziato fit* into the attorney's argument? The reader should never be left to guess why the attorney is discussing a case or what purpose a paragraph serves. More broadly, the reader should not have to extract and piece together the propositions advanced in support of the attorney's conclusion.

The paragraph below tries to rebut the opponent's (Nokia's) argument that reliance is a necessary element of a claim under the California Unfair Competition Law. Every hallmark of a well-written paragraph—including unity, brevity, a topic sentence, logical relations and verbal links between adjacent sentences, and omission of unimportant details—is absent, and the attorney fails to make a coherent argument:

> Nokia relies upon *Cattie v. Wal-Mart Stores, Inc.* with respect to the "reliance" issue. The court in *Cattie* acknowledged that the defendants in that case cited *Pfizer, Inc. v. Superior Court* for the proposition that a plaintiff must both plead and prove that she relied on the false advertising, but also acknowledged that *Pfizer* had been vacated by the California Supreme Court. The court stated that it could look to other authority but acknowledged that there was a split of authority. Nokia cites *O'Brien v. Camisasca Auto. Mfg., Inc., Hall v. Time, Inc.,* and *Buckland v. Threshold Enterprises, Ltd.* for the proposition that "reliance" is an element which must be established with respect to a CLRA claim and a UCL claim. Neither *O'Brien* nor *Hall* referred to the fact that the issue was before the California Supreme Court in *Tobacco II* and *Pfizer v. Superior Court*. On the other hand, *Buckland* stated: "We do not hold that the standing requirement at issue incorporates a requirement of actual reliance. That issue is presently before our Supreme Court." [citations omitted]

Instead of stating propositions that add up to the preferred legal conclusion, the excerpt above asserts propositions lacking any clear relation to the argument at hand:

- "The court in *Cattie* acknowledged . . ."
- "The defendants in that case cited . . ."
- "The court stated that it could look to other authority . . ."
- "Neither *O'Brien* nor *Hall* referred to the fact that the issue was before the California Supreme Court . . ."
- "*Buckland* stated . . ."

A judge is unlikely to take the time to unscramble such paragraphs in search of an argument.

7.2. Take off the IRAC and CREAC training wheels.

First-year law students are commonly taught to organize their legal arguments according to the acronym IRAC (Issue, Rule, Application, Conclusion) or CREAC (Conclusion, Rule, Explanation, Application, Conclusion). Though perhaps useful as starting points for beginners, these formulas oversimplify legal reasoning and tend to produce unconvincing arguments and repetitive prose.

IRAC encourages the poor practice of beginning an argument with an issue phrased as a question, as though a legal argument were a thriller whose ending should not be given away too soon. Instead, begin an argument with the conclusion you hope to establish. A judge can easily infer the issue to be decided from a brief's well-stated conclusion. The "issue" is whether the argued-for conclusion is correct.

CREAC correctly advises the legal writer to begin an argument with the conclusion, but encourages verbosity by requiring an "explanation" of the rule. Only rules that are confusing or disputed should be explained.

CREAC also advises the writer to restate their conclusion at the end of each argument. This leads some law students and lawyers to unnecessarily repeat a statement they just made a few sentences or paragraphs before. Although you wouldn't want an argument to simply trail off, the idea that you must both begin and end every argument with a conclusion implies that the reader will somehow forget the aim of your argument before reaching the end of that argument. If that occurs, you've confused the reader and lost their attention, and fixing that requires more than restating the conclusion.

Law students may also be led astray by an assumption that the items called for by one of these acronyms are equally important. The most important part of a legal argument is the "analysis" portion, in which the attorney shows how the facts and law together lead to the preferred conclusion.

7.3. Craft simple, audience-focused arguments.

Before you start drafting a brief's argument section, brainstorm all the arguments you could make, then decide which you think a judge will find compelling. You can search for research leads and tentative arguments in treatises discussing the relevant law, in cases that were decided in favor of a litigant in your client's position, and by using your experience-honed legal intuition.

All that should occur before you open the word processor. Don't assume, when you've developed a creative argument and found legal support for it, that the argument belongs in your brief. The only argument that will ultimately matter is the one that the judge decides controls the outcome. So the only arguments that belong in a finished brief are those that your judge could reasonably be expected to rely on in deciding the motion in your favor.

Under the principle of judicial restraint, judges usually decide an issue only if they must. The phrase *we need not decide* is one of the most common clichés in appellate opinions. When a judicial opinion wades into expositions that are unnecessary to decide the issues at hand, those statements constitute dicta and seldom create binding precedent.[1]

One application of this principle is that if you are a defendant challenging an element-based cause of action, you may want to focus your attack on the weakest element or two of the plaintiff's claim, rather than on trying to defeat them all.

Delete weak and marginal arguments. An argument is worth making only if it has a realistic chance of persuading the court to decide an issue in your favor. Even then, if you have more than three to five arguments on an issue, some of these should be omitted or—if you need to preserve them for oral argument or appeal—moved to footnotes.

Just as writers are advised to "kill their darlings" by ruthlessly cutting early drafts to sharpen the final document, attorneys must not become too attached to an argument. If an argument turns out to be untenable or weaker than other available arguments, discard it.

7.4. Explain your reasoning and avoid conclusory statements.

The most common substantive mistake in legal filings, as in law-school exams, is making conclusory statements. A statement is conclusory if it asserts a legal or factual conclusion without backing the assertion with an argument. Every time you assert a conclusion in a legal brief, consider whether the conclusion is expected to be disputed by the opponent or questioned by the judge. If so, you need to defend the conclusion by backing it up with an argument. The argument should include the facts, citations to authority, and reasoning that prove the conclusion.

Before we explore some varieties of conclusory assertions found in legal writing and discuss how to avoid them, here's a simple tip you can implement immediately. When in doubt, add "because" statements. Whenever you find yourself stating a disputable conclusion (e.g., "Plaintiff fails to satisfy the summary judgment standard"), follow that statement with *because* and provide a reason.

A simple tell that a statement needs backing is that it uses a legal term or declares that a legal test is met. In the following example, "last clear chance" is a term of art with legal consequences, not an objective description of what occurred:

> Defendant had the last clear chance to avoid the accident.

Suggested revision:

> Defendant had the last clear chance to avoid the accident because he entered the intersection after Plaintiff.

Conclusory appeals to authority

Attorneys often cite or quote cases whose applicability to the current motion is not self-evident or beyond dispute. Simply putting an authority in front of the judge and claiming that it mandates a favorable ruling, as in this example, is not an argument:

> California courts recognize that the FAA controls in cases like this one. *See, e.g., Warren-Guthrie v. Health Net*, 84 Cal. App. 4th 804, 810 (2000).

This excerpt is conclusory because the attorney asserts, without explanation, that a favorable precedent is a case "like this one." This is like asking the judge to do the attorney's job of looking up the case, analyzing it, and determining whether and why it's analogous.

Conclusory fact statements

Statements about facts can be conclusory. In complaints, affidavits, and other filings, attorneys commonly assert legal conclusions as facts. This example from a brief asserts that two terms of art apply but does not explain why:

> Defendant breached the nondisclosure agreement by disclosing Plaintiff's trade secrets to third parties.

The terms *breached* and *trade secrets* are legal conclusions, so the attorney must establish that the information disclosed qualified as a trade secret and fell within the nondisclosure agreement. Another brief makes a similar mistake:

> Defendant improperly downloaded Plaintiff's proprietary information from the secure server.

The phrase *Plaintiff's proprietary information* includes a legal conclusion about ownership; if it is debatable whether the plaintiff owned the information, the plaintiff's attorney must state the facts on which this assertion of ownership is based. Similarly, the modifier *secure* is a legally relevant characterization that must be supported with specific facts.

Sentences like these are neither informative nor persuasive. Rather than *asserting* that a legal test is satisfied, state the underlying facts *showing* that it is satisfied. If reasonable attorneys could disagree about whether those facts satisfy the rule, cite an analogous case to bridge the gap between the facts and the rule. Force yourself to say what you mean and defend your propositions.

Examples

Let's look at two good examples. In the first, the attorney quotes the statutory term *possessed*, states that the requirement of possession is met, and then states specific facts showing that it is met:

> The auto dealership "possessed" the data in its account because it could log in and retrieve the data at any time.

In the next example, the attorney asserts the legal conclusion that Smith spoliated evidence, states the specific facts establishing that conclusion, bridges the logical gap between the facts (Smith deleted relevant text messages) and the conclusion (Smith spoliated evidence) by citing to an analogous case, and in parentheses concisely shows why the cited case applies:

> Smith spoliated evidence by deleting relevant text messages. The messages were preserved only because their recipient "laughed at" them—an action known as a "tapback." *See Mod. Remodeling, Inc. v. Tripod Holdings, LLC* (awarding sanctions because a defendant spoliated evidence by "intentionally deleting the messages associated with the tapbacks that were inadvertently preserved").

Put yourself in the shoes of the judge and opposing counsel—both skeptical readers—when editing your briefs. Asserting vague buzzwords and legal conclusions as though they are objective facts arouses judicial skepticism and creates openings for an opponent to attack.

7.5. Align your arguments with the motion's procedural posture.

Most written motions are made by invoking a procedural rule that allows litigants to file that type of motion. Different motions have different procedural rules that constrain what facts judges may consider and what law they must apply. These procedural rules should be central to attorneys' decisions about how to write briefs supporting or opposing the motion.

Briefs that seem unaware of procedural constraints—for example, motions to dismiss that introduce facts from sources other than allegations in the plaintiff's complaint—put you at risk of losing the court's trust.

Procedural context also affects which authorities you should cite in supporting or opposing a motion. It is more effective to cite cases that were decided either in a similar procedural context or in one that is even less favorable to your side than the current context. For example, if you represent a plaintiff and need cases to cite in opposing a defendant's motion to dismiss, look for cases in which an appellate court reversed a trial court's dismissal order.

If you deviate from this rule and rely on cases involving different procedural standards, alert the judge if there is any risk that they might feel misled. Here's an example of how to do so in a case parenthetical:

> Aeroflot ignores James' citation to the Seventh Circuit case *Sompo Japan Ins., Inc. v. Nippon Cargo Airlines Co.*, which does not relate to removal or subject-matter jurisdiction. *See* 522 F.3d 776, 786–87 (7th Cir. 2008) (holding, in an appeal following a bench trial, that a plaintiff could pursue a setoff claim under Illinois law).

Try to choose favorable battlegrounds for your arguments so that the procedural rules favor you rather than your opponent. That might mean, for example, deferring a challenge to the opposition's claims until trial instead of trying to hit an early home run through a motion for summary judgment. At trial the plaintiff will have the burden of producing evidence for their claims and proving each element of those claims, without the benefit of favorable procedural rules.

Here's another good example, a legal-standard section that uses its space effectively to show that the court has little choice but to grant the motion:

II. Legal standard for Anti-SLAPP fee motions

A party that successfully moves to strike claims under California's Anti-SLAPP statute is entitled to recover their costs and attorney's fees, including the fees incurred in preparing both the motion to strike and a later motion seeking to enforce the statutory fee provision.

Statutory fee provisions are designed "to provide financial incentives necessary for the private enforcement of important civil rights." The Anti-SLAPP statute's fee provision is broadly construed to carry out the legislative purpose of reimbursing a party for expenses incurred in extracting themselves from a baseless lawsuit. [citations omitted]

As with any argument device, emphasizing a favorable standard can be overdone. For example, I have seen plaintiffs' attorneys file briefs opposing motions to dismiss in which most of the brief elaborated on the procedural standard.[2]

Such overlong procedural standard sections conclusorily imply—not by analyzing the complaint's allegations, but by accumulating pro-defendant quotations from judicial opinions denying motions to dismiss—that because the standard is difficult to meet, the defendant has not met it in the current case, so the motion must be denied.

7.6. Keep most rule statements short.

Synthesize, organize, and trim rules, presenting only what the judge needs. Simple rules can often be stated in one or two sentences and backed by a single citation to authority.

With most motions, the applicable law is clear and straightforward. Attorneys arguing those motions are expected not to innovate but to quickly explain to the judge what the applicable rule is and how it applies.

Most rule statements should therefore be concise, and supported by only one cited authority per legal proposition. Quickly proceed to the more important part of your brief, which is explaining to the court how the rule applies to the facts and demands a decision in your client's favor.

An overlong legal standard section may cause the judge to stop reading your brief and start skimming it instead. It could even lead the judge to suspect that you are afraid of arguing the motion on the merits. A rule statement is not by itself an argument.

Here's an effective, single-sentence legal-standard section for a brief opposing a motion to dismiss:

II. Procedural standard

In ruling on a motion to dismiss for failure to state a claim, courts assume that the facts alleged in the complaint are true, then ask whether these facts allege a plausible claim for relief under any legal theory. *See generally Ashcroft v. Iqbal*, 556 U.S. 662, 667–84 (2009).

Rather than writing lengthy legal-standard sections that discuss the law in isolation, it's better to keep those sections short, then elaborate or remind the court of other rules as needed in the argument section while you are applying the law to your case. Here's a good example:

As shown in the Separate Statement of Disputed Responses, HP supplied only boilerplate objections to Walton's requests for admission. But HP cannot object to an entire request for admission unless the entire request is objectionable. Rather, it must object to the part it finds objectionable, then respond to the remainder. Further, when it objects, HP must clearly state the specific ground for each objection and claim any applicable privilege.

HP's responses disregard these requirements. The Court should strike HP's objections and order it to provide complete answers to Walton's requests for admission.

Every trial judge has read innumerable discovery motions, and they may skim sections of a brief that describe standards applicable to such motions. If you are the party moving to compel discovery, however, you want to bring these favorable standards to the court's attention. To that end, apply them in your argument section rather than simply reciting them in a legal standard section.

8 Using Legal Authority

Arguing about the law typically means arguing about written authorities—not about logic, fairness, or policy. If you don't root your arguments in legal authority, a judge may suspect that those arguments lack a legal basis. You'll also probably lose. In a courtroom, appeals to experience, common sense, or other nonlegal grounds cannot defeat sound arguments based on authority.

8.1. Use citations to support your argument, not as a substitute for analysis.

Legal briefs should present the judge with polished arguments that articulate their premises, back them up with citations to apt authorities, and show how they interact to mandate a conclusion.

Instead, some attorneys assert their desired conclusion, then paste in whatever they turn up on Westlaw and say it supports the conclusion.

But they don't walk the reader through their analysis or explain how the cited authorities interact with each other and with the case's facts.

Recall the famous "square peg in a round hole" scene from the movie *Apollo 13*.[1] The astronauts' lives were at risk because the Lunar Module in which they were traveling was not designed to be used by three astronauts at once, and its carbon monoxide filters were overloaded. NASA's engineers had to design a makeshift filter using only the materials available in the module. The lead engineer begins the problem-solving process by dumping all the available materials on the table and saying, "We need to make *this* fit into the hole for *this* using nothing but *that*."

That's as far as many legal briefs go. An attorney gathers research materials and dumps them on the judge's desk—often in the form of long block quotations and string citations—while confidently asserting that the cited authorities mandate a ruling in their client's favor.

The *Apollo 13* scene would be less magical if the engineers had carried the boxes of materials upstairs to their bosses and said, "We haven't put it all together yet, but it's clearly going to work." Instead, they brought their bosses a working filter along with instructions for making it. Everything else was left in the basement.

That is a good model for a legal brief. Judges don't care about your research process or all the interesting sources you read or ideas you had. They care about the legal argument you've crafted and the authority-backed reasons the argument is correct. The authorities are not themselves the argument, and block quotes should not substitute for analysis.

8.2. Understand the hierarchy of legal authority.

Rule statements and other legal propositions should normally be accompanied by citations to a source of law such as a statute or case. But not all authorities are equally strong. To understand what arguments judges are likely to find persuasive, litigators must remain alert to where the sources they use fall on the hierarchy of legal authority. Here is a rough hierarchy:

Tier 1

1. Binding in-jurisdiction cases decided by the jurisdiction's highest court
2. The language of an applicable and enforceable contract
3. The language of an applicable statute

Tier 2

4. Binding in-jurisdiction cases decided by intermediate appellate courts

Tier 3

5. Landmark legal treatises or other strong secondary sources[2]
6. Persuasive but nonbinding federal appellate cases, especially on issues of federal law
7. Persuasive federal district court cases, especially on issues of federal law

Tier 4

8. General legal principles such as maxims of equity[3]
9. Persuasive appellate cases from other states
10. Other secondary sources such as law review articles

Move down the hierarchy only if you have a reason to do so—because you couldn't find any binding authority on point or because a persuasive authority is especially helpful.

Rarely cite unpublished cases, even if your jurisdiction allows it. And avoid cases with negative subsequent history. Citing a case that has been depublished, vacated, or superseded can seriously damage an attorney's credibility, so it's imperative to verify that the cases you cite remain good law.

Rarely cite concurrences, per curiam opinions, or dissents. When you do, you'll need to add a parenthetical such as "(Smith, J., conc.)" qualifying the authority.

Another thing to consider when selecting cases is whether the case could help your opponent. Some cases contain unhelpful language that may show up in the opponent's next filing. Others contain supportive language but were ultimately decided for the "wrong" side—that is, the side whose position mirrors that of your opponent. To find out, you'll need to read the cases you cite. Many attorneys skip that step, but doing so can be costly.

8.3. Be strategic about how many authorities you cite.

The fact that you found a relevant case does not justify citing the case. As with everything else in your brief, each citation you include must serve some communicative purpose and add useful information. It should advance your argument without duplicating the work of other citations.

Think strategically about what authority you need to make the best possible arguments while keeping the brief succinct. Every rule statement and other legal proposition in your brief should be presumed to require at least one citation.

Here are some guidelines for determining how many authorities to cite for a proposition and to what extent you should discuss those authorities.

For each legal proposition in your brief, consider how likely it is that the judge will be skeptical of the proposition or that your opponent will challenge it. If you expect it to be challenged, estimate how strong a challenge might be. The answers influence these decisions, which must be made for each proposition:

- Will you explain the proposition and any reasoning or analysis that underlies it, or just cite an authority and move on?
- If you have more than one supporting authority available, how many should you cite?

For each authority you cite, ask:

- Should you mention the authority in the main text or in a footnote?
- If the authority is a case, should you discuss the case's facts or reasoning? If so, should you discuss these in the main text or in an explanatory parenthetical?

At one end of the spectrum, there are propositions that cannot reasonably be disputed. These include, for example, well-known procedural rules and rules derived directly from binding precedents. You can ordinarily support these with a single citation to a binding authority, with no explanatory parenthetical or discussion needed.

For example, this is a straightforward proposition supported by one unexplained citation:

> An order granting an anti-SLAPP motion is reviewed de novo. *See Flatley v. Mauro*, 39 Cal. 4th 299, 325 (2006).

By contrast, your most controversial propositions might need to be supported by several citations. You will need to explain your reasoning and show why the authorities you cite compel the result you want.

Your decision about how much to support a proposition should be guided, in part, by the readability principles discussed throughout this book: concision is better than verbosity, and unnecessary details should be omitted. Simplicity makes for better prose and better arguments.

The quality of your citations matters more than their quantity. Even with contested propositions, one strong citation is better than three weak ones. Judges prefer simple arguments that point them to one binding case that they must apply.

To determine whether adding another case citation to an already-supported proposition would improve your argument, consider (1) where the source sits on the hierarchy of legal authority and (2) how legally and factually similar the cited case is to your case.

Every argument is different, but a common way to defend tricky propositions is to establish a broad rule or framework by citing a case from the highest court in the jurisdiction, then add citations to cases lower in the hierarchy that are closely analogous to your case. The secondary citations show that your case falls within the broad rule.[4]

8.4. Minimize string citations.

String citations—long chains of citations, often unexplained, that purport to back a proposition—are rarely helpful. As suggested in the previous section, it's better to cite just enough authorities to establish a proposition.

Consider supporting a proposition with a string citation only if the proposition is contested and you have no binding authority on point (or it is unclear whether the authority you cite resolves the issue).

Providing string citations to support obvious or uncontested points of law has the counterproductive effect of making the point seem controversial. Here's an example of an unhelpful string citation that amounts to a research dump:

> A demurrer tests the complaint alone, not the complaint combined with a defendant's premature evidentiary submissions. *See, e.g., Del E. Webb Corp. v. Structural Materials Co.*, 123 Cal. App. 3d 593, 605 (1981); *Cruz v. County of Los Angeles*, 173 Cal. App. 3d 1131, 1134 (1985); *Fremont Indem. Co. v. Fremont General Corp.*, 148 Cal. App. 4th 97, 115 (2007).

This string citation is inappropriate because the proposition in the first sentence is well known and uncontroversial. The citation is made even more unhelpful by the absence of parentheticals or other text explaining why each cited case matters. If you must use a string citation, use parentheticals to provide some factual context for each case or otherwise explain why the citation is nonredundant.

Here's a good example of a string citation being used to establish a controversial point of law—note the use of parentheticals to make clear why each cited case contributes something to the argument:[5]

> Even if the $1,165.19 charge could be construed as "rent," provisions purporting to collect unearned "future rent" are void as penalties. *See, e.g., Ricker v. Rombough* (1953) (holding that "rent acceleration" clauses causing unearned future rent payments to become due upon breach are void as penalties); *250 L.L.C. v. PhotoPoint Corp.* (2005) (holding that a security deposit may not be applied to "future rent"). [citations simplified]

Another reason this example's string citation is helpful is that the main support for the proposition is a case decided in 1953. Old cases are sometimes worth citing, but they give opponents an easier target and may make the judge wonder whether they are still good law. Bolster them with citations to newer authorities showing that the law has not changed.

8.5. Create context before discussing cases.

Most citations in a legal brief do not require any explanation or factual context because the proposition they support is straightforward, well known, and unlikely to be contested. Judicial opinions often contain standalone rule statements such as recitations of a claim's elements. If you insert that rule statement in your brief and cite the case where you found it, you are effectively treating the cited case as a mini-treatise—a repository of written rules. You are not arguing that the case is analogous, only that it accurately describes a rule.[6]

That said, for controversial propositions, rule statements for which a case provides only indirect support, or rules whose applicability is disputed, you'll often need to provide some factual context from the cases you cite to assure the reader that they apply.

Above all, consider the relationship between the cited case and the proposition it supports. If that relationship is attenuated, you'll need to mention the cited case's facts. For example, if you're suggesting that a precedent is analogous to your case, you must describe the facts and law that make the precedent analogous.

To see what is wrong with the following example, ask yourself how the cited cases support the preceding propositions (you'd have to do the research yourself to find out):

> The relief Carbonara seeks would simply require federal courts to decide an issue—whether the state court's failure to consider his ability to pay violated his constitutional rights—that has already been fully litigated in the state courts and is collateral to the merits of his pending prosecution. *See Courthouse News Service v. Planet*, 750 F.3d 776, 789–90 (9th Cir. 2014); *Tarter v. Hury*, 646 F.2d 1010, 1013 (5th Cir. 1981).

At a minimum, both of the citations in this excerpt should have explanatory parentheticals. Note that it's impossible for the citations to directly support the stated proposition because Carbonara wasn't a party to those earlier cases. Accordingly, the attorney needed to explain how those citations applied.

Only discuss a precedential case in the body of your brief if it's central to your argument and warrants discussion. Before discussing it, say why it matters and what proposition it supports. Avoid starting paragraphs with a case-centric topic sentence such as "In *Smith v. Jones*, the plaintiff . . . ," or at least wait until you've created context for the discussion and motivated the reader to care about what happened in the case. Here's a good example from an appellate brief:

> Courts have rejected arguments that fee awards should be reduced because the prevailing party could have negotiated more or bargained away their rights.
>
> In *Goglin v. BMW of N. Am., LLC*, for example, the Court of Appeals rejected an argument that a fee award should be reduced because the plaintiff could have achieved their objectives by accepting an early settlement offer. The offered settlement had included a general release and confidentiality clause, neither of which were required by the applicable law, and the plaintiff had a right to pursue their legal rights without accepting those compromises. [citations omitted]

Judges should never have to wonder why they should care about details they encounter in your brief, including details about what happened in a different case.

8.6. Use parentheticals effectively.

Explanatory parentheticals—in which an attorney briefly comments on a citation in the citation itself rather than in the main text—can be used to quickly explain why you are citing a case without disrupting the thread of your argument. They are especially useful when a citation provides only indirect support for a proposition but is not important enough to discuss in the main text.

The following excerpt from a brief shows an effective use of parentheticals. Google is arguing that copyright holders should be forced to litigate their claims about Google Books case-by-case, rather than in a class action. In the first paragraph, Google cites cases without mentioning their facts or supplying parentheticals; this is appropriate because the citations' role is to support incontestable rule statements drawn directly from Supreme Court cases. In the second paragraph, Google moves down the hierarchy of authority and cites district court cases that are factually on point and support Google's position. Google uses parentheticals to summarize those cases' key facts and holdings:

> The Supreme Court has consistently rejected "bright-line rules" in the fair use context, *Campbell v. Acuff-Rose Music*, and has noted Congress's recognition that "each case raising the fair use question must be decided on its own facts," *Sony Corp. of Am. v. Universal City Studios, Inc.*
>
> This often requires a fine-grained analysis that can lead to different fair use conclusions even about uniform uses of substantially similar works. *See, e.g., Cambridge Univ. Press v. Becker* (reaching opposite fair use conclusions about 37-page excerpts from two books because one book earned significant digital licensing income and the other did not); *id.* at *76, *161 (finding use of 41 pages equaling 5.8% of a book fair because the portion "was decidedly small," but use of a shorter excerpt from a shorter book not fair in part because the excerpt comprised 8.28% of the total work, which the court found "not decidedly small"). [citations simplified]

It bears emphasizing that the parentheticals in this example show how the facts in the cited cases led to those cases' holdings. This strengthens the citations by showing that Google is not relying on dictum.

Another good use of parentheticals is to expand on a legal proposition:

> Equity's labels for the provisions are irrelevant; what matters is how they operate. *See Garrett v. Coast & S. Fed. Sav. & Loan Ass'n.* ("In order to evaluate the legality of a provision for late charges we must determine its true function and character."). [citation simplified]

In the example below, the attorney cites *Adkinson* as the primary support for a proposition. But *Adkinson*, it turns out, was discussing a different statute than the one at issue. Therefore, the attorney—in a move that strengthens their argument and preserves their credibility—includes a parenthetical clarifying that *Adkinson* was discussing a different statute. Then, in the same citation sentence, the attorney cites a second case (*Hickman*) with a parenthetical showing that it makes no difference that *Adkinson* involved a different statute:[7]

> A defendant commits healthcare fraud only if they execute (or try to execute) a scheme to defraud. Merely *devising* such a scheme is insufficient. *See Adkinson* (discussing the bank-fraud statute, 18 U.S.C. § 1344); *Hickman*

(using the bank-fraud statute to interpret the healthcare-fraud statute because the statutes' "language and structure are almost identical"). [citations simplified]

Phrasing the parenthetical

Unless consisting entirely of a quotation, most explanatory parentheticals should begin with present participles such as *holding, stating, discussing,* or *affirming.* These convey important information while keeping your parentheticals parallel.

Choose the participle carefully, because it signals whether you're relying on the earlier case's holding, a rule statement untethered from the holding, or dictum. A few examples are given in table 8.1.

Table 8.1   Examples of participle use in parentheticals

Participle	Poor example	Good example
holding	*Bouvia v. County of Los Angeles,* 195 Cal. App. 3d 1075, 1083 (1987) (holding that "fees should not, in the interest of justice, be paid out of any recovery").	*See also Richmond,* 29 Cal. 3d at 475 (holding that even where six percent of the class opposed the class action, the "small number should not be sufficient to defeat the motion for certification").
stating	*See Bustamante,* 141 Cal. App. 4th at 210–11 (stating that no contract had been formed because the condition precedent of getting funding from third parties, an essential term, had not occurred).*	*See Lockett v. Ohio,* 438 U.S. 586, 604 (1978) (stating that the "qualitative difference between death and other penalties calls for a greater degree of reliability when the death sentence is imposed").
none	The harmless-beyond-a-reasonable-doubt standard applies here. *People v. Ashmus,* 54 Cal. 3d 932, 965 (1991) (state-law test for error is equivalent to *Chapman* test).	*See Warth v. Seldin,* 422 U.S. 490, 511 (1975) ("Even in the absence of injury to itself, an association may have standing solely as the representative of its members.").

* This parenthetical describes the court's holding, not a mere statement.

A court's *holding* is the court's decision coupled with the essential facts and reasoning that led to the decision. But the concept of a holding is nebulous, and sometimes reasonable attorneys disagree on what a case's holding is. When in doubt, use *stating* rather than *holding*.

8.7. Use the full menu of available citation signals.

Citation signals such as *see* are the introductory terms of a citation sentence that show the relationship between the cited authority and the proposition for which it is being cited.

Every law student learns the citation signal *see*, and attorneys could go through their careers without experimenting with the others. But citation signals allow you to efficiently give the judge information they need to evaluate a citation's strength and relevance. Lawyers who do not understand the different signals risk inadvertently misleading the court.

Table 8.2 explains the available citation signals.[8] Experiment with some of the lesser-known ones in your filings.

Table 8.2   Citation signals in legal writing

Signal	Meaning	Example
No signal	The citation directly supports the preceding proposition, is the source of a quotation, or provides bibliographic information for an authority referred to in the main text.	That dictum is also wrong. It is not supported by the authority *Boardman* cited—*Ohio Bureau of Emp. Services v. Hodory*, 431 U.S. 471 (1977)—which makes no mention of an express-statement rule, instead referring only to a State "voluntarily choos[ing] to submit to a federal forum." *Id.* at 480.
See	The citation directly or indirectly supports the preceding proposition. The more attenuated the support, the more important it is to include an explanatory parenthetical.	This Court has long held that a defendant cannot "knowingly" make a false statement unless they have actual knowledge of its falsity. *See United States v. Williams*, 685 F.2d 319, 321 (9th Cir. 1982) (holding that 18 U.S.C. § 922(a)(6)—which makes it a crime "knowingly to make any false or

Table 8.2   Citation signals in legal writing (continued)

Signal	Meaning	Example
See (continued)		fictitious oral or written statement" in connection with a firearm purchase—requires proof of actual knowledge of falsity, not mere "reckless disregard for truthfulness").
See also	The cited authority buttresses a proposition. Use only when the proposition is nonobvious (justifying multiple citations). Include a parenthetical explaining why the second citation adds information and is not superfluous. Also, consider omitting this citation signal and just using a semicolon after the preceding citation.	The opinions offered by Stover and Winters are even clearer examples of improper lay opinions; they could only have been given by trained accountants. *See United States v. Morales*, 108 F.3d 1031, 1039 (9th Cir. 1997) (en banc) ("[T]he subject matter at issue—bookkeeping principles and [the defendant's] grasp of them—was clearly beyond the common knowledge of the average layperson" and thus within the scope of Rule 702); ***see also*** *City of Tuscaloosa v. Harcros Chems., Inc.*, 158 F.3d 548, 564 n.17 (11th Cir. 1998) ("[A]ccounting expertise is among the sorts of technical and specialized expertise the use of which is governed by Rule 702.").
See generally	The cited authority provides background information or a general overview of a rule or doctrine.	All Craft's requests seek documents relevant to the subject matter of this dispute, which involves Point's ouster of his partner Craft from the potato business they cofounded in 2019. ***See generally*** First Am. Compl.
But see	The cited authority contradicts the proposition.	In an untenable attempt to avoid TUTSA preemption, K2 narrows its fiduciary duty claim to encompass "confidential information, such as personal information about vehicle owners," but not "trade secrets." ***But see*** *Super Starr Int'l, LLC v. Fresh Tex Produce, LLC*, 531 S.W.3d 829, 843 (Tex. App. 2017) (rejecting a similar argument).

Cf.	Short for Latin *confer* ("compare"). The cited authority is not directly on point but provides indirect or analogous support for a proposition. Include an explanatory parenthetical.	Smith's objection that the word *collected* is somehow vague and ambiguous is evasive. *Cf. Deyo v. Kilbourne*, 84 Cal. App. 3d 771, 783 (1978) (stating that if an interrogatory is somewhat ambiguous, but the nature of the information sought is apparent, the responding party must provide an appropriate answer).
But cf.	The cited authority casts doubt on the proposition or contradicts it indirectly (or by analogy).	The cause of action generally accrues when the employee learns or should have learned of the union's decision. *See, e.g., Demars v. General Dynamics Corp.*, 779 F.2d 95, 97 (1st Cir. 1985). *But cf. Barina v. Gulf Trading & Transp. Co.*, 726 F.2d 560, 562 n.2 (9th Cir. 1984) (suggesting that a claim does not accrue until the last date at which the union could have brought the grievance under the collective bargaining agreement).
Compare ...with ...	The cited authorities are useful to compare with each other; comparing the authorities supports or clarifies the proposition.	*Compare* RJN Exh. R (signed lease from Tulip Properties to Redgroup as attached to Sharp's cross-complaint) *with* Sharp Decl. Exh. D (same signed lease, but with blanks for the start date and duration term).
Accord	The cited authority agrees with an authority referred to in the main text.	We agree with the *Woods* court that the term "stranger" means one who is not a party to the contract or an agent of a party to the contract. *See Woods*, 129 Cal. App. 4th at 353; *accord Mintz*, 172 Cal. App. 4th at 1604 ("[C]orporate agents and employees acting for and on behalf of a corporation cannot be held liable for inducing a breach of the corporation's contract.").
Contra	The citation contradicts the proposition. *Contra* is rarely used. But one effective use of it is to point out contradictions in an opponent's filings.	In his declaration, Cheney admits for the first time that a deposit had been made to place the property in escrow before he was brought in to complete the purchase. Cheney Decl. ¶ 7; *contra* Cheney Cross-Compl. ¶ 47 (claiming that he purchased the land with $1.2 million of capital provided solely by himself).

Table 8.2   Citation signals in legal writing (continued)

Signal	Meaning	Example
. . . *e.g.,*	Short for Latin *exempli gratia*, meaning "for example," this signal indicates that the cited authority is just one of many that could have been cited.	Neither witness was qualified to testify about any accounting issues, let alone a GAAP violation, and neither supported their conclusory statements. *See, e.g., United States v. Hamblin*, 911 F.2d 551, 558 (11th Cir. 1990) (reversing a conviction because "intuition cannot substitute for admissible evidence when a defendant is on trial").

8.8. Write arguments in your own words.

An attorney's role is to develop an argument consisting of a legal conclusion supported by authority-backed reasons. This requires synthesizing and explaining the results of your research.

Write briefs in your own words, paraphrasing most of what you might otherwise quote. Then weave in quotations as needed when the specific language used in the cited source advances your argument, or where paraphrasing would be inappropriate.[9]

Here's a good example of a pro-plaintiff legal standard section that uses only paraphrasing, not quotations (in the original, each sentence is followed by a footnote containing a citation):

> A demurrer admits all facts pleaded in the complaint as well as facts inferable from the complaint and its attachments as liberally construed, however improbable these may be. Any competing inferences are drawn in favor of the plaintiff. The accuracy and precision of the allegations, and any difficulty the plaintiff may face in proving the case, are irrelevant. A demurrer must be overruled if, taking the facts alleged in the complaint as true, the plaintiff may have a right to relief under any possible legal theory. [citations omitted]

Supply context for the quotations you introduce to ensure that the resulting text is logical and cohesive. Here's an example from a brief in which the sentence preceding a quotation (in bold) falsely advertises the quotation's contents, and the quotation itself bears no obvious relation to its surroundings:

> There is no question that the *Knapp* decision was mainly based on evidence presented to the Court in the form of declarations from Mr. Vickers and Mr. Kenny. **The Court in *Knapp* basically acknowledged as much at p. 943 as follows:**
>
>> The evidence produced in connection with the motion for class certification confirmed the lack of commonality and representations (or omissions) by AirTouch to members of the proposed class regarding its service plans. Substantial evidence showed AirTouch used several channels to market the service plans. AirTouch used print advertisements in newspapers and magazines.

Pause before pasting text from a case into your brief. Think of how you would explain what you've found to a client or partner over the phone. You wouldn't normally quote entire paragraphs from the source; instead, you would convey the gist of what you found, telling the listener what it all adds up to and why they should care.

Use quotations only when the specific language used in the source matters—for example, when you're quoting a statute, contract, or opposing party's statement—or when a source explains a concept especially clearly.

In the example below, the brief unnecessarily quotes a court's description of a legal rule. By quoting rather than paraphrasing, the lawyer has introduced clutter in the form of verbosity and alterations:

> "Evidence Code section 220 creates an exception to the hearsay rule for [an] admission of a party," but "does not define when a declarant-party's extrajudicial hearsay statement becomes *relevant* to be admissible against such party under the personal admission exception to the hearsay rule." *People v. Allen*, 65 Cal. App. 3d 426, 433 (1976) (emphasis in original).

Suggested revision, paraphrasing the point and adding the citation signal *see*:

> Although a party's statement may be exempted from the hearsay rule, that has no bearing on whether the statement is relevant. *See People v. Allen*, 65 Cal. App. 3d 426, 433 (1976).

Quotations can often be simplified. Rather than quote entire sentences, trim unnecessary language and replace it with alterations and ellipses (so long as doing so does not make the quotation misleading).

Additionally, try to weave quotations into your own sentences, which improves the document's flow and cohesion. A brief that includes many extensive quotations from other sources may lack an authorial voice or sense of unity.

Judicial opinions are not statutes, so the exact language the opinion's author used to express an idea or describe a legal rule might not matter. Consider restating the rule in your own words. Here's an example of a poorly phrased rule statement, drawn from a judicial opinion, that should be rephrased and simplified:

> In resolving the ambiguity, courts will adopt an interpretation that yields reasonable results and reject interpretations that yield unreasonable ones.

Suggested revision:

> In resolving ambiguities, courts reject interpretations that lead to unreasonable results.

Avoid the "cleaned up" parenthetical.

Appellate lawyer Jack Metzler proposed using the parenthetical "(cleaned up)" to replace minor alterations such as changes in capitalization and omission of internal ellipses, quotation marks, footnotes, and citations when quoting a case that itself quotes a different case.[10] The practice has been endorsed by some legal-writing experts and judges. Even so, I advise against it because of its unfamiliarity and its potential for leaving the reader to wonder what exactly has been changed.

Opposing attorneys cannot always trust each other to make intellectually honest arguments and provide fair, accurate quotations from the sources they cite. Many attorneys misquote and mischaracterize their sources or fail to accurately record every alteration in their quotations. I fear that if the "cleaned up" technique continues to proliferate, the technique will be misused, leading to even sloppier quotation practices.

8.9. Use block quotations judiciously.

Block quotations can be helpful, but they cannot substitute for the writer's own analysis. They are also prone to overuse and usually include more language than needed.

The best use for block quotations is when you want to quote an extended passage (more than fifty words) from a contract or statute. Another good use is when you are quoting from trial or deposition transcripts.

Even then, delete as many words and sentences as you can, replacing them with ellipses. When you quote a contract or statute, omit language that refers to inapplicable exceptions or that cross-references irrelevant provisions.

For example, suppose you want to cite Cal. Civ. Code § 1951.2(a), which begins:

> Except as otherwise provided in Section 1951.4, if a lessee of real property breaches the lease and abandons the property before the end of the term or if his right to possession is terminated by the lessor because of a breach of the lease, the lease terminates.

If the exception referred to doesn't apply, remove the clause referring to that section when you quote the statute:[11]

> [I]f a lessee of real property breaches the lease and abandons the property before the end of the term or if his right to possession is terminated by the lessor because of a breach of the lease, the lease terminates.

This provision can be condensed even further if only one of its two alternatives occurred. The tenant either abandoned the property *or* had their right to possession terminated by the lessor, but probably not both. The situation that didn't happen can be omitted from the quotation and replaced by an ellipsis:

> [I]f a lessee of real property['s] . . . right to possession is terminated by the lessor because of a breach of the lease, the lease terminates.

Introduce block quotations with a lead-in sentence that stands alone as a complete assertion. Then follow the block quotation with a wrap-up sentence that helps the reader further understand why the passage was quoted. Encapsulating quotes in this way makes the text more cohesive.

8.10. Format citations correctly but minimize clutter.

Correct citation formatting is a mark of professionalism and attention to detail. Law students who participate on journals get a lot of experience with citation formatting, but others may have to make a point of learning it themselves.

I recommend learning the *ALWD Guide to Legal Citation*, which is better organized than *The Bluebook* but uses the same rules. Avoid other legal citation formats, such as the *California Style Manual*, unless your jurisdiction mandates them.

Citations should contain only the information needed for the reader to identify the source and evaluate its position in the hierarchy of authority. Omit the following citation signals, none of which are relevant to a source's strength:

> **Cert. denied.** A court's denial of certiorari or other discretionary review does not signal approval of the lower court's decision.

> **As amended.** The fact that an opinion you cite amends an earlier opinion is irrelevant.

> **Reh'g denied.** Petitions for rehearing are routinely denied, so the denial of a petition for rehearing does not strengthen an opinion's authority.

> **Opinion of.** The name of the judge who wrote a majority opinion likewise does not usually affect its authority. If you're citing a plurality opinion, just add the parenthetical "(plur. op.)."

Here are two examples of citation clutter found in legal filings. Everything in bold should be deleted:

> *See State v. Marshall*, 123 N.J. 1, 66 (1991), **cert. denied, 507 U.S. 929 (1993)**.

> *See In re Mego Fin. Corp. Sec. Litig.*, 213 F.3d 454, 458 (9th Cir. 2000), **as amended (June 19, 2000)**.

Secondary case reporters

Every jurisdiction has official and secondary reporters for published cases. A legal citation manual can help you identify the official reporter (the one to cite). In the following example, the attorney unnecessarily cites a secondary reporter:

> In *Jue v. Smiser*, 23 Cal. App. 4th 312, 28 Cal. Rptr. 2d 242 (1994), the court said that reliance must be established at the time the initial contract was struck, and that it is not necessary that a plaintiff establish continuing reliance until the contract is fully executed to maintain an action for damages. 23 Cal. App. 4th at 317.

Here's a revision that removes the secondary citation while using plain language and leading with the proposition rather than the case name:

> To prove fraudulent inducement of a land-sale contract, the plaintiff need only show that reliance existed when the contract was formed—not that reliance continued until the contract was fully executed. *See Jue v. Smiser*, 23 Cal. App. 4th 312, 317 (1994).

"Citing" and "quoting" parentheticals

"Citing" and "quoting" parentheticals are rarely needed. Legal cases routinely cite and quote each other, so these parentheticals multiply citations without adding information.

Only use a "citing" or "quoting" parenthetical if the secondary case is somehow important for your argument. This most often occurs when you cite a lower court's opinion that relies on a higher court's opinion, and when the legal proposition you are defending may be disputed. Here's a poor example:

> Because this matter comes before the Court on a motion to dismiss, the allegations below in Plaintiffs' Second Amended Class Action Complaint ("Second Amended Complaint") are taken as true. (Doc. #15); *Ashcroft v. Iqbal*, 556 U.S. 662, 678 (2009) (internal citations and quotation marks omitted) (quoting *Bell Atl. Corp. v. Twombly*, 550 U.S. 544, 570 (2007)); *Zink v. Lombardi*, 783 F.3d 1089, 1098 (8th Cir. 2015).

Suggested revision:

> The Second Amended Complaint alleges the following facts, each of which must be taken as true in ruling on a motion to dismiss:[1]
>
> [1] *See Ashcroft v. Iqbal*, 556 U.S. 662, 678 (2009).

A good example appeared in an appellate brief filed in the Eighth Circuit. The brief's "citing" parenthetical makes sense, because the main case is an Eighth Circuit case that cites a Supreme Court case:

> Under controlling Eighth Circuit law, this Court "review[s] all aspects of the imposition of sanctions under an abuse of discretion standard." *Harlan v. Lewis*, 982 F.2d 1255, 1259 (8th Cir. 1993) (**citing *Chambers v. Nasco, Inc.*, 501 U.S. 32, 55 (1991)**).

Another good use of a "citing" parenthetical is to bolster a case you cite by showing that the decision applied a highly regarded source of law. This suggests that the cited authority followed legal tradition and is not an outlier. Here's an example:

> Because the deputies did not act unreasonably or excessively for purposes of the Fourth Amendment when executing the warrant, they cannot be held liable for assault under Kansas law. *See Dauffenbach v. City of Wichita*, 657 P.2d 582 (Kan. App. 1983) (under state tort law, an officer may use reasonable force to carry out an arrest) (**citing Restatement (Second) of Torts § 132 cmt. a (1965)**).

It's necessary to bolster a cited authority only when the legal rule for which you're citing it is disputed. Otherwise, parentheticals like these just take up space.

9 Legal Storytelling

9.1. Think like a storyteller.

9.2. Select your facts carefully, omitting most nonessential details.

9.3. Use labeling to make abstractions more concrete.

9.4. Call parties by their names, not their procedural labels.

9.5. Avoid unnecessary definitions.

9.6. Simplify or omit dates and locations.

9.7. Keep the procedural history section short but persuasive.

Behind every legal dispute is a story about people in conflict. If the conflict cannot be resolved informally, it may lead to a lawsuit. Most plaintiffs do not find themselves in court because they see an opportunity for profit; rather, they feel forced to sue because without suing, an intolerable status quo will continue.

The stakes of litigated disputes can be enormous. Winning or losing a lawsuit may determine whether a company survives or is forced into bankruptcy, for example. If any civil litigation seems boring or abstract, it may be because the attorney who filed the lawsuit has lost sight of the dispute's origins as a high-stakes conflict between real people, or does not know how to convey the human drama of the dispute on the page.[1]

Strong fact sections tell concise, compelling stories that are closely tied to the brief's legal analysis and make a favorable result seem inevitable and just.

9.1. Think like a storyteller.

Conflict is the essence of litigation. It's also, in film and literature, the essence of plot. Litigators, like novelists, are in the business not just of performing legal analysis but also of telling stories and challenging the stories told by others. A litigator's skill in selecting and narrating a dispute's facts to weave them into a compelling story can determine whether their client prevails.

Most of the advice you would hear in a fiction-writing workshop applies to fact sections in legal briefs. Good stories show rather than tell, allowing the reader to draw their own conclusions rather than telling them what to think. They describe settings with enough detail for the reader to visualize them. They describe fleshed-out characters with whom the reader can empathize, and they help the reader get to know these characters through dialogue and other devices. They choose descriptive details that compress information, give rise to inferences, and carry emotional power. They describe sequences of events within a narrative, omitting extraneous and tedious events such as time spent asleep. They minimize vagueness and abstraction, aiming to create a visualizable mental world and invite the reader in.

There are two main differences between a work of fiction and a fact section.

First, while fiction writers may invent or change facts to improve the story, attorneys must make do with the facts available in the current procedural context—allegations in the complaint or evidence admitted at trial, for example. Attorneys also often need to include "bad facts" that are legally relevant but difficult to reconcile with the story they want to tell. But the need to work with a limited set of facts and refrain from making anything up is true of creative nonfiction, so the difference between literature and legal storytelling is less significant than one might think.

Second, attorneys must select and arrange facts so that they fit within the brief's legal argument. The desired legal conclusion should seem to flow naturally from the facts.

Humans are constantly creating and sharing narratives to make sense of events; we are born storytellers. An attorney's role includes telling their client's story in a way that is consistent with the facts but aligned with the desired outcome. Write your fact section with the mindset of a creative-nonfiction writer, out to tell the truth while keeping the reader interested and subtly motivating them to side with your client.[2]

9.2. Select your facts carefully, omitting most nonessential details.

You've heard the message throughout this book: legal documents should include only essential details—details that serve some argumentative or rhetorical purpose. Drop weak arguments, unnecessary citations, needless digressions, nonessential modifiers, and anything else that does not help the reader.

Nowhere is this principle more important than in the fact section of a brief. Fact sections swollen with pointless details are a disservice to the client, as these details obscure the client's story.

In persuasive fact sections, as in good literary fiction, every detail is there for a reason. Usually, that means the detail is relevant to the legal rules the judge must apply. If a fact is legally immaterial,[3] mention it only with good reason: because it provides needed context, adds color to or fills gaps in a narrative, undermines an opponent's story, suggests that justice is on the client's side, or serves some other rhetorical purpose.

Playwright Anton Chekhov put it best, giving rise to the narrative principle known as Chekhov's gun: "If in the first act you have hung a pistol on the wall, then in the following one it should be fired. Otherwise, don't put it there."

Identifying legally relevant facts

Whether a fact matters to a legal argument depends on whether it intersects with the applicable rule. Suppose the speed limit on a residential street is 25 mph. If a red 2022 Dodge Challenger, driven by a man in his mid-forties wearing business-casual attire, blasts down the street at 47 mph while its driver sings off-key to Carly Rae Jepsen's "Call Me Maybe," the driver has violated the speed limit.

Most of the facts just stated have no legal relevance because they have nothing to do with a relevant rule. Only two items from the anecdote matter to the law:

1. **Legal rule:** The applicable speed limit was 25 mph.
2. **Fact bringing the driver's conduct within the legal rule:** The driver was going 47 mph.

An attorney writing a fact section about this event should be disinclined to mention anything but the driver's speed, since none of the other facts are legally relevant. But this is a guideline, not a rule.

Suppose the speeding scene portrayed above turned into a personal injury case because the driver hit a pedestrian. The pedestrian's complaint might mention some legally extraneous facts to humanize the characters and add narrative color as part of telling a story.

Two poor examples below show the importance of selecting telling details (and omitting unimportant ones) in crafting a compelling narrative.

In the first, excerpted from a response brief on appeal, virtually every detail is irrelevant. It illustrates common facts that attorneys often can't stop themselves from including—who represented whom; whether someone was served; which documents were filed, when, in what courthouse, and before which judge; and so on:

> In June 2013 Appellant filed in the Contra Costa Superior Court a Summons and Petition for a Dissolution of Marriage. Respondent was served with process after which a timely response was filed on August 29, 2011. It was on July 21, 2012, that Appellant and Respondent appeared, each with the assistance of privately retained counsel, whereupon counsel for Respondent announced the fact a settlement had been reached. Petitioner agreed to each and every one of the terms of the stipulation.
>
> It was on May 8, 2013, that Petitioner did, by and through her attorney, file a request for entry of judgment of dissolution of marriage nunc pro tunc, which request was accompanied by the declaration of Matt L. MacKinnon, Esq., Attorney at Law for Appellant. It should also be noted that the request for entry of judgment included the fully executed stipulation of the parties which was also signed by the Presiding Judge. Judgment was entered as requested and filed May 18, 2013.

The issue on appeal was whether a stipulated divorce judgment may be appealed if a party changes their mind. None of the facts in the example matter other than that the divorce proceeding ended with a stipulated judgment.

Attorneys sometimes share irrelevant facts, then admit their irrelevance and leave them in the brief rather than deleting them, as in the second example:

Through a separate Partner Program, publishers authorize Google to display much larger excerpts from works. More than 44,000 publishers have authorized inclusion of 2.4 million books in the Partner Program. Users search and view books in the Partner Program through the same web interface used to search and view snippets of other books in the Google Books corpus.

The Partner Program is not at issue in this case.

Now let's look at two good examples, adapted from opposing briefs in a Supreme Court case.[4] Note which details each party uses to tell their story, develop a case theme, suggest that the equities are on their side, and set the stage for a legal argument. In the first excerpt, the plaintiff focuses on the case's facts as they allegedly emerged at trial:

Plaintiff Jesse Williams's Statement of the Case

This case involves a massive market-directed fraud driven by high-level decisions to deceive customers and endanger their health to generate enormous profits. It constituted one of the longest-running, most profitable, and deadliest frauds in the annals of American commerce. Jesse Williams became highly addicted to cigarettes, smoking three packs a day of Philip Morris's "Marlboro" brand, using industry denials (as Philip Morris intended) to rationalize his continued smoking. He died of lung cancer in 1997.

For at least 40 years, Philip Morris knew that cigarettes cause lung cancer and that millions of American smokers, about half of whom were its customers, were addicted to the nicotine in cigarettes. In an effort to maximize profit, Philip Morris either publicly denied this knowledge outright, saying more research was needed, or disingenuously reassured its customers it would never jeopardize their health.

In the second excerpt, the defendant describes the same facts briefly and anesthetically. They choose a telling detail ("three packs of cigarettes a day") to suggest that the plaintiff had only himself to blame, then pivot to discussing procedure:

Defendant Philip Morris USA's Statement of the Case

Jesse Williams began smoking cigarettes in 1950. After 1955, Williams smoked Marlboros, which are manufactured and marketed by Philip Morris. Williams eventually smoked three packs of cigarettes a day. He was diagnosed with cancer in 1996 and died in March 1997. Alleging negligence, strict product liability, and fraud, Williams's widow sued Philip Morris.

At trial, plaintiff mounted a wide-ranging attack on Philip Morris's conduct over a period of 50 years. In closing arguments, plaintiff urged the jury to punish Philip Morris not only for the harm caused to Williams but also for unidentified harms suffered by countless other, unidentified Oregon smokers who were not before the court and whose individual circumstances were never presented to the finder of fact.

As these examples show, attorneys have many ways to subtly promote their case themes when describing what happened in a dispute. Good attorneys can tell compelling stories without embellishing or hiding the facts, openly appealing to emotion, or slipping into argument (none of which are acceptable in a fact section). They can make strategic choices about which facts to emphasize, which details to include, which words to choose, which level of abstraction to adopt, and whether to describe an event by painting a scene or providing a summary.

9.3. Use labeling to make abstractions more concrete.

Abstractions weaken prose and interfere with narratives because they do not occur in scenes and cannot be easily described or visualized. If you can write about something tangible (e.g., a judge in a courtroom) rather than an abstraction (e.g., the legal system), do so. If you need to use the abstraction, give it a name.

Replacing numbers with names

Avoid using nonessential numbers in your fact section. Large numbers, especially non-round numbers, are hard to think about, visualize, or remember. This is particularly true of arbitrary numbers (e.g., bank account numbers, inmate numbers, and other identifiers) that function as names rather than representing quantities.

In the following poor example, the attorney bores and confuses the reader by referring to lawsuits by their case numbers (using "M122091," a case number, to identify a property tax lawsuit) and cluttering the text with record citations that should be moved to footnotes:[5]

> M122091 would be irrelevant to this action, but for two factors. Although the attorneys kept working on the settlement to open the escrow called for by the 2011 Settlement, including negotiation over the format and terms of the new note (2011 Settlement P 5, CT 1092), and drafts were exchanged (FACI, Ex. 1-2, CT 357-360), the instruments were not finalized by December 2015, as memorialized in a letter from Appellant-Beneficiaries attorney to present counsel. (Girard Decl. p. 23, Ex. 4 (highlighted text), CT 1261, 1269-70.) Present counsel meanwhile was in the process of withdrawing from M122091 over a fee dispute, and the negotiation "petered out" inconclusively. M122091 was later dismissed. Respondent Mahan had no role in M122091.

Instead of calling the case by its number, the attorney could have labeled it the "Tax Case":

> At that time, the Firm was withdrawing from the Tax Case due to a fee dispute, and the parties were unable to negotiate a settlement. Mahan had no role in the Tax Case, which was later dismissed.

Naming legal concepts

Assigning names to legal concepts and clusters of concepts can be a powerful rhetorical technique. We do this all the time without thinking about it: a "corporation" is a legal concept, but most people don't think of it that way. Instead, most imagine a mental substitute, such as an office building.

You can use such thought patterns to your advantage. If you're trying to establish that cofounders of a business formed a partnership by operation of law, for example, give the partnership a name, as in this good example from a complaint:

> In 2018, friends and entrepreneurs Bob Dawson and Larry Solano saw an opportunity to get in on the ground floor of Vermont's booming apple industry. They began pursuing city and state licenses and set up a farming and delivery company. The two brought on a third partner—investor Thomas Tucker—to help realize their dream, and the partnership known as "BLT" (standing for "Bob, Larry, and Thomas") was born.

You can also name clusters of concepts. Another good example, a point heading in an appellate brief filed in a criminal case, groups and names the counts on which the defendant was convicted:

> The District Court's erroneous jury instruction requires a new trial on the **healthcare-fraud counts**.

This strategically powerful move makes it easier for a judge to follow your argument and creates the possibility that a favorable ruling on one issue may lead to a favorable ruling on related issues.

9.4. Call parties by their names, not their procedural labels.

Labels like *Plaintiff* don't make for compelling characters. Instead, humanize the parties by using their real names, especially if there is only a single plaintiff or defendant in the lawsuit.

Exceptions apply. If you represent a corporate defendant against a sympathetic plaintiff named Rose, for example, you may want to maintain a dry and impersonal tone by referring to "Plaintiff" instead of "Rose."

Additionally, when multiple parties are on one side of the case, it may be easier to refer to them as a group. You may also have strategic reasons for doing so. In one antitrust case, for example, the plaintiff attempted to lump the subsidiaries of a global manufacturer together by referring to them by their parent company's name, suggesting that they operated as a single entity. The defendants insisted that the subsidiaries be treated separately so that each would be held responsible only for its own actions, not those of its affiliates.

When you use procedural labels like *Plaintiff* and *Defendant*, take care to capitalize them appropriately. If you refer to the plaintiff as "Plaintiff," you are effectively turning that term into a proper noun. You can't then say "*a* Plaintiff," since you are talking about a specific plaintiff.

9.5. Avoid unnecessary definitions.

Attorneys often create defined terms as shorthand to avoid having to repeat a long term or phrase. But some shorthand names are self-evident and do not require a definition. Below are three poor examples (with unnecessary definitions in bold) in which there was no chance that the reader would be confused:

> Defendant Ford Motor Company, Inc. (**"Ford"**) asks the Court to dismiss Plaintiff's Second Amended Complaint with prejudice.

> Under the Federal Rules of Evidence, only relevant evidence is admissible. *See* Fed. R. Evid. 402 (**"Rule 402"**).

Since definitions aim to convenience rather than confuse the reader, use only one defined term for each concept. Don't do this:

> Appellant, one of the named defendants below, Earl T. Sugar, **will be referred to herein interchangeably as "Appellant" or "Sugar."** The Estate of Starr T. Sugar is from time to time referred to as the "Estate." Appellee, the plaintiff below, H&M HYDRO PUSH, INC., d/b/a H&M PURITY SYSTEMS, a Florida corporation, **will be referred to herein interchangeably as "Appellee" or "H&M."**

Finally, create a defined term only if you intend to use it more than twice. Don't make the reader learn new vocabulary they won't use.

9.6. Simplify or omit dates and locations.

Attorneys tend to describe dates and locations more specifically than they should. For example, consider the sentence "Apple was founded on April 1, 1976, in Cupertino, CA." Does the exact date of Apple's founding matter? Does the city in which it was founded matter? If not, simplify. Write "Apple was founded in 1976" or "Apple was founded in California in 1976."

Here's a poor example:

> This legal dispute concerns liens against the above-mentioned single-family dwelling **located at 1805 Laguna Street, Seaside, Shasta County, CA 93955.**

Suggested revision:

> This dispute concerns liens against a home in Shasta County.

It's hard to conceive of any use a judge might have for the property's exact address, so it shouldn't go in the brief. If it must be included, put it in a footnote. If several homes must be distinguished, call this one the "Laguna Home."

Dates are also abstractions that can't be visualized, and they tend to pile up; if a brief mentions one date, it probably mentions several. Every time you use a date, ask whether the reader needs it; if so, ask whether it can be simplified. Here's a revisable example:

> By way of background, Respondent purportedly received a letter on **May 30, 2013,** from the Innocence Project.

Suggested revision:

> Respondent purportedly received a letter in **May 2013** from the Innocence Project.

Readers usually need to know the contents of a smoking-gun email, not that the defendant sent it at 11:46 p.m. PST on November 21, 2019.

One way to help readers follow along is to use relative dates to show how events are sequenced and spaced apart. Before introducing a sequence of events in your fact section, orient the reader in time by starting with an absolute date such as "November 21, 2019," then use relative dates such as "the same day" or time markers such as "immediately" for later events.

This is a good example:

> In **June 2004,** when Jones was copied on an internal routing form enclosing the cover letters and expense reports, he forwarded them to the lawyers. Smith **promptly** responded that "our team has been activated on the BH expenditures." **Two weeks later**, McFarland sent Jones a legal memorandum about 80/20 reporting.

Here's another good example, this one using only relative dates:

> More than **sixteen months after** filing its declaratory judgment action challenging the patents, Transco made a startling new allegation: it claimed that its president had publicly distributed samples of oil-resistant filters at a trade show **fifteen years earlier.**

Using relative dates allows you to map a timeline of events for the reader, sparing them from having to do it themselves. This is an example of the principle that readable texts make clear how details interrelate and show how each new detail fits into what the reader already knows.

"On or about"

Don't say "on or about" if you know the exact date. Many legal writers habitually use that phrase, especially when drafting lawsuit complaints. But if a personal injury complaint says that the key accident occurred "on or about December 15, 2020," this communicates that the attorney couldn't be bothered to learn the exact date on which the accident prompting the lawsuit occurred.

Here's a poor example:

> **On or about February 24, 2014,** the Borrower executed a Promissory Note effective as of **February 25, 2014,** whereby the Borrower promised to pay to the order of Marin the principal sum of $750,000.00 with interest thereon computed from the effective date of the Note at the rate of 3.75% per annum.

Suggested revision:

> **On February 24, 2014,** the Borrower and Marin executed a Promissory Note for $750,000, with an annual interest rate of 3.75%. Interest began accruing **the next day.**

9.7. Keep the procedural history section short but persuasive.

Unless you want the court to focus on procedural matters rather than the dispute's underlying facts, discuss the case's procedural history in a separate section or subsection from the facts, and keep the discussion as short as possible. Procedural history sections are often the most boring parts of a brief, and you don't want the judge's eyelids to droop before they make it to your argument.

An exception applies if your argument, or the opponent's, turns on procedure. If so, include strategic details such as quotations from trial transcripts or rulings that are designed to bolster or cast doubt on the challenged proceeding.

In this good example, a litigant used a procedural history section to bolster a lower court's ruling:

> After engaging in a searching review of the record, the Michigan Supreme Court in 2007 found Stark's misconduct to be "extreme and outrageous" as well as "extraordinarily reprehensible, by any measure of which we are aware."

In another good example, the litigant is appealing a lower court's decision on procedural grounds, so they use the procedural history section to suggest that the court made mistakes:

> After finding that Johnson violated his probation, the court held a sentencing hearing over several days in 2007. During this hearing, no expert testimony about Johnson's future dangerousness was offered.
>
> The court rejected all the recommended sentences. It imposed a sentence of life imprisonment for the armed burglary and 16 years for the attempted armed robbery. The court explained that Johnson was incapable of being rehabilitated or deterred from future crimes and that protecting the community by incapacitating him was the court's only option.

PART III   Process

10 The Mental Game of Writing

Even professional writers struggle to start, continue, and finish writing projects. Writing is strenuous work that requires full concentration and lots of mental energy. As with other high-stakes and high-effort tasks, we tend to put it off.

Mental obstacles to writing take countless forms and can crop up anytime in the drafting process. Once we overcome our initial resistance and sit down to write, we may struggle to finish. Then, wishing to put the task behind us, we may resist revising. Or, fearing rejection, imperfection, or the sense of aimlessness that sometimes follows a major project, we may find excuses to continue revising rather than finishing and turning in the draft.

This chapter demystifies the writing process while offering suggestions for overcoming procrastination, perfectionism, fear of failure, and other sources of resistance.

10.1. Think critically about obstacles you encounter.

When writers encounter difficulty, they sometimes feel paralyzed and unable to move the project forward. Monitor your emotions and notice when you feel that way; the feeling is often followed by an instinct to escape into distraction by switching to a less important task. Try to catch and analyze feelings of resistance before you give in to them.[1]

Review your writing habits and workflow with the mindset of an investigator out to identify and solve problems.[2] Replace any sense of being generally stuck or overwhelmed with an awareness of specific problems, sources of discomfort, and inefficiencies, as a therapist or writing coach might encourage you to do. Can you adjust your process to mitigate aspects of writing that you dread or tend to avoid? Can you enlist help?

10.2. Break projects into chunks and take them one step at a time.

Every large project is a collection of small tasks. When you're working, think in terms of the smaller tasks rather than the more distant goal of a finished document.

Break tasks down until they feel manageable and nonthreatening. In a summary judgment brief, for example, each section in your outline can be thought of as a separate writing task. Think of the task at hand as "Draft the claim preclusion section" rather than "Draft the summary judgment motion." If needed, you can break down the task even more: instead of "Draft the claim preclusion section," you can instruct yourself to "Write a paragraph distinguishing the *Smith* case." If you're away from your keyboard, you can set yourself a task such as "Record a voice memo with ideas for what I want to say in the fact section."

Devote your best writing time, the time when you expect to have the most energy and fewest interruptions, to the more important and challenging components of the writing project. But continue to take small steps forward even when you lack energy. In those times, take care of your project's "low-hanging fruit"—easier subtasks such as drafting a legal-standard section, plugging in rule statements, formatting citations, or handling simple but necessary tasks such as preparing proposed orders. When you end a writing session, write down the next action you can take to move the draft forward.[3] This makes it easier to resume the project later.

10.3. Complete timed sessions of focused writing.

Focus on process rather than outcome while you are writing. If the task before you is to fill a blank page, it is counterproductive to worry about anything else. Focus on keeping your cursor moving until the writing session is complete.

Along with dividing daunting tasks into manageable subtasks, you can divide tasks into chunks of time. Rather than say "I'm going to work on my research memo," for example, say "I'm going to work on my research memo *for fifteen minutes*." Then set a timer and focus until the timer expires, at which time you can give yourself a break.

The practice of completing timed sessions of focused work is called the *Pomodoro Technique*. No matter how overwhelmed you feel, or how tempted you may be to turn away from a writing task and check your email, ask yourself: "Can I bear to work on this draft for ten minutes?" You probably can. So set your timer for ten minutes and get to work. Chances are that when the ten minutes are up, you'll be in a state of flow and willing to continue working. If not, that's fine too; take a break, then set another ten-minute timer.

Visual timers can help you use the Pomodoro Technique by making it easier to perceive the passage of time. My favorite is called the "Time Timer" (shown in figure 10.1). You set the timer for the duration you want to work, and then you can observe it in your peripheral vision as its red indicator shrinks. When the timer reaches zero, it beeps to signal that it's time for a break.

Figure 10.1. Time Timer.

When you finish a focused writing session, take a moment to experience the small victory. Completing the session is an accomplishment, no matter how much progress you made or how much work remains.

10.4. Budget your time realistically.

Take time at the start of a project to estimate how long it will take. Do so from the perspective of a project manager. Think conservatively, without relying on hope, a positive mood, or magical thinking. Plan for exigencies and commitments that will be competing with this project for your time, energy, and attention.

Periodically take breaks and zoom out from whatever section you are working on to look at the overall document and check whether you are investing your writing time appropriately, focusing on the most important parts of the draft. Don't dwell too much on any one section.

In long projects, watch for thresholds after which you experience diminishing returns. By getting too caught up in one part of a larger project (or even one case in a portfolio of cases), you risk neglecting other parts of the project, overworking the project as a whole in relation to the client's budget, or running out of time to get lower-priority sections into a serviceable state so that you can submit a finished document on time.[4]

Manage your overall expectations for the document and reality-test your sense of its importance. For litigation filings, ask: Does this filing have a realistic chance of materially improving the client's position? Does it need to be as elaborate or thorough as first envisioned? Are you sure the client wants to pay you to work on it for ten hours, or would they be satisfied with five?

If you work as part of a team, these are not problems to try to solve alone. Communicate with your colleagues and don't be afraid to seek help. If you get stuck on any part of a project, try talking through what you want to say, delegating, or dividing the work.

10.5. Avoid the trap of perfectionism.

Monitor yourself for perfectionism and keep your self-demands in check. In litigation, the main priority is often completing a document on time rather than writing flawless prose. Some tasks (a client update or meet-and-confer letter to opposing counsel, for example) just need to be completed quickly and cleared from your desk.

Even if you hold yourself to the highest standards of writing, and your firm uses proofreading software and dedicated editors, your document will not be perfect. It may contain embarrassing typos or other errors that somehow escape round after round of revisions. I sometimes joke that I do my best editing right after I file a brief.

All that is fine. Unsightly and unpolished briefs do not amount to malpractice, but missed filing deadlines may. In legal writing, "done on time" is almost always more important than "well argued" and "well written," though it's best to budget your time and get the help you need to accomplish all three.

10.6. Manage procrastination.

One belief implicit in every decision to procrastinate is that if you don't work on the project now, things will be fine. The project can be safely put off until another day. You can catch up on lost time tomorrow, over the weekend, or next month.

Not all deferrals of work amount to procrastination. It is often true that a project need not be worked on today. Since we can only work on one task at a time, projects that are not time-sensitive must often be put off. But sometimes we fib to ourselves about whether we can safely postpone a project. When we want to work on a task today and ought to do so today, yet still fail to make time for it, *that* is procrastination. And if procrastination creates mental stress or forces you to cut corners on an important project, it becomes a problem that must be addressed.

Dreaded writing projects share two traits with necessary surgeries. First, if the project is mandatory, any unpleasantness associated with it will need to be suffered at some point. Second, the writing process may not be as painful as you fear. Upon close inspection, many writing difficulties turn out to be related to discrete, manageable problems rather than to the project as a whole.

Since you need to do the work at some point, it may help to "feel the future" and empathize with your future self. Will your attitude toward the project be different then, when your earlier procrastination has turned the project into an emergency that must override other commitments? Or will you feel even more negative about the work at that point?

10.7. Start writing projects as soon as you can.

Start work on a writing task as early as possible. A useful mantra is to "touch the task" immediately, taking a small step to get it under way. Don't let it become a monster in the closet that feels scarier the longer it is kept in the dark.

Our minds tend to confuse *starting* a project with *doing* the project. But starting is just the first step, and it need not be painful or time-consuming. One benefit of disaggregating a project—breaking it into manageable chunks—is making clear that the project's beginning is a discrete, nonthreatening step in a longer process.

You must ultimately break through your resistance and put some words on the page, but that isn't necessarily the first step. To prepare yourself to type those difficult first words, try writing thoughts on a legal pad, dictating ideas into a smartphone app while commuting, talking through your ideas with a colleague, finding templates or models, or priming your brain by reading about the same topic.

Starting immediately on a writing task has four benefits. First, the only way to finish is to start. Second, we tend to feel more negative about and fearful of tasks we put off. Third, starting allows your mind to work on the material unconsciously between writing sessions. Fourth, starting a draft earlier tends to mean that you'll finish it earlier, giving yourself time to put it through several rounds of revision.

The problem of getting started—sitting at one's desk, shifting away from one's default state of non-writing, and starting to put words on the page—crops up not only at the beginning of a project but anytime you step away from it to work on something else. One problem with being constantly interrupted is that it forces you to reset your mind and turn back to the blank page again and again, creating new opportunities for mental resistance and sapping your willpower.

10.8. Use templates and models to jump-start your document.

Starting drafts with a blank page can feel intimidating. Consider starting with templates and models, such as motions written by attorneys whose writing you respect.

You can find examples of every kind of legal document by searching Lexis or Westlaw. To increase the chances that you'll find a good example, add the name of an elite firm or litigator to the search query. For example, in Lexis, you could set the source-type field to "Briefs, Pleadings, and Motions" and then search for *WilmerHale "motion for summary judgment"* to find summary judgment briefs written by the prestigious firm WilmerHale. Collect samples that you might be able to use as starting points in future projects.

Another option is to use formbook treatises and practice checklists, such as *American Jurisprudence Pleading and Practice Forms Annotated.* These are useful as starting points and to check for common provisions or points you've forgotten to include.

Avoid wholesale copying from formbooks, though; clients pay you to use your legal judgment, not to sell them downloaded boilerplate. For example, if you don't understand why a contract provision is there or how it operates, either find out and revise it to make its purpose and operation clear or get rid of it. Rewrite each provision you use in your own words, cutting every nonessential paragraph, phrase, and word.

10.9. Optimize the physical side of writing.

Writing is a physical as well as mental act, so note how you are using your body as you work. Learn and follow ergonomic recommendations, such as keeping your wrists straight, your hands at or slightly below the height of your elbows, and your monitor at eye level.[5] If you work while seated, take frequent breaks to stand up and walk around.

Consider buying a standing desk and an antifatigue standing mat. I own a motorized standing desk that can be raised or lowered with a button. When I lived in a small apartment without room for a standing desk, I used two workarounds: an elbow-height bookshelf that I kept empty, and an elevated laptop stand that could be placed on my desk. Whenever I use a standing desk, my body somehow senses that it's time to get down to business and make focused progress.

Move around and vary your writing environment. Try working outdoors. At a minimum, go outside often to breathe deeply, reorient yourself in time, and make yourself feel grounded. Nature can calm and stimulate your mind.

Any change of scenery can stimulate you and make you feel more alert. Writing from an unfamiliar location can trick your brain into overcoming writer's block and help you generate new ideas. I keep a cheap Bluetooth keyboard in my car so that I can type from anywhere, using my smartphone as a miniature tablet.

Finally, consider giving your body something else to do while you type. Find something to do with your feet, and with your hands when they aren't typing. I carry a stress ball around and hold it when I'm thinking. I also have a rolling foot massager near my desk to keep my feet busy. Some writers like to sit on yoga balls or similar devices to force themselves to stay upright and alert.

10.10. Try to get in a state of flow.

Psychologist Mihaly Csikszentmihalyi invented the concept of "flow" to describe the feeling of becoming fully absorbed in one's work and losing track of time.[6] A colloquial phrase expressing the same concept is "being in the zone."

When writing comes easily, the writer is experiencing flow. This is much more pleasant and productive than dragging a draft out of yourself sentence by sentence while thinking of something else you'd rather be doing.

There are two competing recommendations about what to do if you manage to get into a state of flow. Some argue that you should set a timer and stop working when the timer ends, even if you are still in the flow state, so that you end the session on a positive note. Others advise capitalizing on the flow state by getting as much done as possible until you run out of energy. I take the latter view. When I'm completing a timed Pomodoro session and the timer goes off while I'm in a flow state, I ignore the timer and keep working.

Although most writers can't turn flow states on and off at will, there are ways to make them more likely. The subsections below discuss how you can try to get into a flow state by completing prewriting breathing and visualization exercises and avoiding multitasking.

Use breathing and visualization exercises.

As a logic-minded skeptic and someone who struggles to relax, I'm not naturally receptive to advice to meditate or perform mindfulness exercises. But the science is clear: such practices improve concentration and performance. They are indispensable tools for writers because they can help you set anxiety aside, defeat writer's block, and enter a flow state.

If you search online for "breathing exercises" or "mindfulness," you'll find many resources, including apps, to help you incorporate these concepts into your writing routine. I like the simple Apple Watch app "Breathe," for example. The app offers a one-minute breathing routine in which you inhale deeply for a few seconds, then exhale.

Mindfulness exercises usually involve breathing deeply while noticing minutiae such as tension in your shoulders or the veins on a leaf. Many breathing exercises encourage you to inhale through your nose and exhale through your mouth. One advises tensing and raising your shoulders as you inhale, then relaxing and dropping them as you exhale.

The related technique of *visualization* is commonly used by musicians, athletes, and other performers. Visualization involves mentally picturing yourself taking some action before you do it. If you're resisting a writing task, close your eyes and envision yourself opening a word processor and writing the first paragraph. This takes some of the fear out of that action and mentally prepares you to do it.

Avoid multitasking.

Multitasking is incompatible with flow. The essence of flow is complete absorption in a single activity so that other concerns fall away. Multitasking involves doing the opposite.

Cognitive science says humans cannot perform two or more tasks simultaneously if each requires conscious thought. When people appear to be multitasking, they are just rapidly shifting their attention between tasks. Such task-switching makes you less productive and exacts a mental cost by requiring you to hold too much in your working memory and constantly refocus. It's better to do one thing at a time, without distractions.

10.11. Eliminate, plan for, and pivot from distractions.

Distractions are stimuli that make a claim on your attention and tempt you to divert your focus. Minimizing visual, auditory, and mental distractions is essential to getting into and staying in a flow state.

Different writers prefer different environments, so figure out what works for you. For some people, minimizing distractions means finding or creating the equivalent of a library carrel. But that doesn't work for everyone. I like working near open windows in natural light and don't want silence, preferring instrumental background music and the white-noise buzz of a café.

Auditory and visual distractions

When you're ready for focused work, minimize auditory distractions by silencing notifications, turning off your phone, and closing the door. Tell your colleagues when you'll be unavailable because you have scheduled time for focused writing. Then make the most of those opportunities by disconnecting from everything except the draft.

Try to minimize visual distractions, too. Keep your desk surface free of clutter so that you don't see reminders of anything but the task in front of you.

Simplify what you see on your computer monitor when you write. Make your editing software full-screen and hide features that are irrelevant at the drafting stage. In Microsoft Word, for example, you can use Focus Mode to hide everything except the page.

Technological distractions

For most contemporary writers, the biggest distraction of all is the internet. It constantly tempts us with dopamine rushes and makes us fear we'll miss something important if we don't click notifications the moment they arrive. The internet has also accelerated the already stressful pace of legal practice; many attorneys, especially junior attorneys, feel obliged to be constantly available and instantly responsive.

Most dangerously, the internet can give us the illusion of being productive. We can turn from our writing to click through cases on Westlaw, check the latest headlines, network with someone on LinkedIn, or browse Google Scholar or Wikipedia. These are valuable activities, but they often pull us away from more important tasks like moving drafts toward completion. They also train our brains to resist long-form reading and other solitary activities that require extended focus.

To write productively, you must control your internet use. Force yourself to use the internet as a tool, rather than allowing it to govern when and how you work.[7]

If the internet is making you unproductive, there are many things you can do other than berate yourself and pledge to do better. You can turn off the connection, use an old computer whose sole purpose is drafting, write with pen and paper, set your emails and notifications to be delivered in scheduled batches, or use internet-blocking and time-tracking programs such as FocusMe and RescueTime.

Mental distractions

You may need to tame mental distractions, too. For example, try not to carry your to-do lists around in your head, taking up valuable working memory that ought to be reserved for your writing project. Rather than trying to remember tasks, write them in a planner and put your appointments in a calendar.

Set periodic reminders before each meeting or deadline and use countdown apps to tell you how many days you have before something is due. Create a system that you can trust to remind you of appointments and deadlines at the relevant times so that your mind can temporarily forget about such obligations and focus on writing.

Other mental distractions include anxiety, worry, fear, and associated negative thoughts that interfere with writing:

- "I'll never finish this before the deadline."
- "We should never have taken this case."
- "The judge won't even read this brief."
- "I'm just not a good writer."
- "I'm not interested in this topic."
- "This job isn't a fit for me."
- "I should be working on the *Jones v. Smith* brief instead of this."

Whenever thoughts like these pass through your mind, they threaten to pull you out of the flow state in which you can enjoy writing and do your best work.

It is sometimes impossible to forcibly suppress negative thoughts, but try writing them down when they occur. If you feel a sense of anxiety about something, note it on a "worry list" to attend to later, after your writing session is over.

.   .   .   .   .

Even if you've gone to some lengths to create a focused writing environment—you've silenced your devices, closed your email and web browser, and told your colleagues that you'll be unavailable—some distractions and interruptions will pierce your defenses. But you have some control over how much time, focus, and mental energy they divert from your writing project. Squash them as quickly as possible and reorient yourself to the writing session, refusing to let it be derailed.

One distraction often leads to another. If you disrupt your writing session to take a phone call or check your email, those tasks can remind you of other items that demand your attention. Stop that cascade the moment you notice it. Turn away from whatever is distracting you, take deep breaths, remind yourself of your intention for the writing session, and then return your focus to the page.

As an exercise, make an inventory of common distractions that pull you away from writing. Consider the steps you can take to prevent them and mitigate their effects. Try the "if this, then that" strategy, making plans like these:

> "**If** I get discouraged about how much I still have to write to finish the document, **then** I'll remind myself that at this moment, I only need to write the paragraph in front of me."

> "**If** I start editing and backtracking as I write the first draft, **then** I'll remind myself to keep my pen moving and defer revision until later."

> "**If** I suddenly remember an upcoming deadline in another case, **then** I'll make a note to deal with it after my writing session."

In short, writing is a demanding, energy-intensive activity that requires your full attention. Writing while distracted tends to be a miserable and inefficient experience that results in inferior work. You will be most efficient if you set aside competing tasks until your writing session is over.

10.12. Follow a systematic writing workflow.

Every published book started as an idea and a blank page, then was pains-takingly drafted one sentence and paragraph at a time. Once the draft was done, it went through many rounds of revision. The polished appearance of a litigation filing similarly disguises the way it was created.

A writing workflow can help free you from the need to decide what to do next each time you sit down to work. Such decisions use mental resources that would otherwise be available for writing. And if you trust your process and know what steps lie between the current draft and a finished document, you may feel less overwhelmed, removing a common mental obstacle to productive work.

Brainstorming, researching, drafting, revising, and formatting involve different mental processes, so trying to do them all at once is inefficient. I recommend the following workflow, which expands on what Bryan Garner calls the "Flowers paradigm" (after its creator, composition teacher Betty Flowers).[8]

Phase One: Prewriting research and brainstorming

1. **Research**. You won't be able to outline or draft a legal document until you do enough research to understand the relevant facts and law (at least in broad outline). For contracts, you'll need to know the transaction's essential terms and what the client hopes to achieve. For litigation documents, you'll need to understand the case's record as well as the applicable procedural and substantive law.

   Specific research needs, such as the need to distinguish an important case or find better authority for an argument, often arise later in the writing process. But you will need to get a basic handle on the matter before you start writing.

2. **Conduct a pre-draft brainstorming session**. Brainstorm ideas for your draft—every point you might want to make, stray thoughts or worries about the draft, potential avenues of research, counterarguments you might rebut, and so on. There are no bad ideas at the brainstorming stage, so suppress the instinct to self-censor. If you're working with a team, consider using software to allow teammates to propose ideas anonymously.

   Brainstorming is nonlinear and benefits from free association between unconnected ideas. Allow one thought to spark another. It helps to capture ideas in different formats, print and digital. These might include "mind maps," scribblings on a legal pad or whiteboard, voice memos recorded on a phone, or transcribed dictations.

Phase Two: Outlining

3. **Decide which points to make and skip**. Once you've generated ideas, you'll need to weed out the ones that are not important or persuasive enough to justify space in your draft. Most ideas generated in the brainstorming session should be discarded.

4. **Create an outline with tentative point headings**. Once you've decided which points to make, put them in order and organize them into a logical structure with nested headings. Your headings need not be polished at this stage; placeholders are all you need.

Phase Three: Initial drafting

5. **Quickly complete a first draft**. Write one section at a time, drafting the most important sections first and saving big-picture sections (such as the introduction and conclusion) for last. Keep your pen moving. Use placeholders such as *[CITE]* when you get stuck or have ideas that might draw you away from your current thread. Most importantly, defer editing, formatting, and polishing; don't let them interrupt your flow.

Phase Four: Revising

6. **Revise and polish the draft**. Improve the draft through successive rounds of revisions, editing "from the outside in" by handling large-scale issues first and deferring wordsmithing and line edits.

7. **Design the document**. The visual appearance of your documents matters, but formatting should be the last step in the writing process.

Writing habits are hard to change, so make a point to practice this workflow.

Steps can sometimes be compressed, grouped, or skipped in the interest of time. If your brief is due in three hours and hasn't been started, it may be smarter to chug a coffee and start typing right away, channeling your inner Jack Kerouac, on the theory that a disorganized filing is better than a late filing.[9]

But if you find yourself stuck during a legal writing project, consider whether you are working on the wrong step of the process and whether you've fulfilled that step's prerequisites. Perhaps you started drafting prematurely, choosing the wrong arguments or structure, and need to backtrack.

10.13. Write "shitty first drafts" without backtracking to edit.

After you understand your main argument and have done enough legal research to get started, produce what Anne Lamott calls a "shitty first draft."[10] What matters at the drafting stage is not getting things right; it's getting words on the page.

This is not the time to edit, wordsmith, second-guess yourself, or go down a rabbit hole of research. Your sole task at the drafting stage is to complete a first draft, however terrible it may be. Don't reread or revise what you've written until the draft is done. Just keep writing.

10.14. Edit in stages, working on large-scale issues first.

Your early drafts will need to be overhauled before being filed or delivered to a client. This section offers suggestions for thorough and systematic editing.[11]

Train yourself to be detail-oriented while editing. Aim for excellence while adjusting your expectations to the time you have available and the importance of the task. Try to improve every argument, section, paragraph, sentence, and word in your draft. Don't tolerate spelling, grammar, citation, or formatting errors.

Since time is scarce, you'll often need to prioritize. Prioritize substance over style while understanding that style matters more than most lawyers assume. As always, the rules of professional ethics—particularly the duty to not misstate the law or otherwise mislead the tribunal—override any competing considerations.

.   .   .   .   .

Most writers edit by starting at the beginning and reading through the document, making changes as they go. But it is more efficient to edit in planned stages.

The keys to efficient editing are to make large-scale revisions first and to focus on one type of problem at a time. I suggest editing in the following order:

Phase One: Document-level edits

1. **Argument strength**. For legal briefs and other persuasive-writing tasks, have you selected your best arguments and discarded the rest? Are your arguments adequately explained, supported by authority, and persuasive? Is a court likely to accept your main argument and grant the relief you request? Have you adequately supported every statement of law, especially contested ones, with apt citations to authority?

2. **Audience**. Is your draft's tone, length, and level of detail appropriate for the audience? Have you put the reader's needs first? For example, a letter to a client usually should not include every nuance that you turned up in your research; the client is probably looking instead for practical, business-minded advice.

3. **Organization**. Is the overall outline of your document logical? Are your sections and paragraphs logically sequenced and coherent? Is each section and paragraph internally unified (focused on one point)? Have you provided context before details? Have you built organization structures (such as lists) for the information you convey? Have you allocated space in your draft in proportion to the importance and complexity of the various sections?

4. **Overall concision**. Have you kept within any page limits and deleted every unnecessary argument, idea, citation, paragraph, and detail to make your draft tight and respect the reader's time and energy?

Phase Two: Section and paragraph edits

5. **Unity and coherence of sections and paragraphs**. Does all the material in a section pertain to a single topic identified in the section's heading? Does each sentence in a paragraph relate to the paragraph's main point, and have you made that point clear in a topic sentence?

6. **Transitions**. Does each paragraph have a clear link to the preceding and following paragraphs? Is the same true for adjacent sentences? Are there any jarring shifts that might cause the reader to wonder why they are suddenly reading about a new topic? Have you given the reader enough context to understand the significance of every detail?

Phase Three: Sentence edits, citation checking, and proofreading

7. **Sentence-level clarity and style**. Have you omitted unnecessary sentences and made the remaining sentences clear and easy to read? Have you varied your sentences' lengths, considered rhythm and emphasis, and frontloaded most sentences with the main subject and verb? Have you deleted every unnecessary word and condensed bloated phrases?

8. **Citations**. Have you cited only published cases that are still good law, included correct pincites, provided parentheticals when helpful, and used proper citation format?

9. **Grammar and punctuation**. Have you thoroughly proofread and cite-checked your document? If you need clarification on grammar or usage, have you sought help from a reference book?[12] Have you read your drafts aloud and had a computer program read them to you? Have you had an editor review your draft?

If you edit line by line before you've completed large-scale edits, you may end up pointlessly refining text that should be discarded.

10.15. Defamiliarize your draft to see it more objectively.

When writers edit just after drafting, the ideas they had while drafting remain fresh in their minds. This can cause them to see what they *meant* to communicate rather than what they wrote.

We want to see our draft from the perspective of a reader encountering it for the first time. This requires distancing ourselves from the text. Here are a few ways to do so:

Give yourself time between drafting and editing. When you finish drafting a section or document, set the draft aside for a few hours (or days) before editing it. This is one more reason to start your writing tasks early.

Print your documents before editing. Many writers find that they are more likely to catch errors if they edit printed documents. It also helps to review drafts on different screens, such as laptops, tablets, and phones.

Read your drafts aloud (and have them read aloud to you). Your ear can catch what your eye misses. By hearing your prose, you will be more likely to notice typos, odd rhythms, and clumsy sentences by stumbling over them yourself. Microsoft Word has a "Read Aloud" feature. You can also try text-to-speech apps, which read aloud your documents.[13]

11 Writing with Technology

11.1. Use software to improve your prose.

11.2. Use dumpfiles to help you revise fearlessly.

11.3. Set up text expansion.

11.4. Learn common keyboard shortcuts.

11.5. Go beyond the basics with Microsoft Word.

11.6. Use templates and styles to format documents.

11.7. Consider using text editors rather than word processors for early drafts.

Writing technologies are the lawyer's equivalent of carpentry tools, but few attorneys take full advantage of them. This chapter introduces you to software features and productivity tricks that many attorneys do not know. It is intended not to serve as a how-to manual but to give you a sense of what is possible. Many online resources are available to show you how to use the techniques I discuss.

Many people are afraid of learning new software or mistakenly assume that productivity strategies like those discussed in this chapter are too difficult to use. Don't let such fears get in your way. Stretch your comfort zone and use the tools available to speed up your workflow.

Technology changes quickly. You can find updated tips and software recommendations on this book's website (www.elegantlegalwriting.com).

11.1. Use software to improve your prose.

Software can help you identify grammar errors and consider style revisions. One general-purpose editing tool is Grammarly (figure 11.1). An

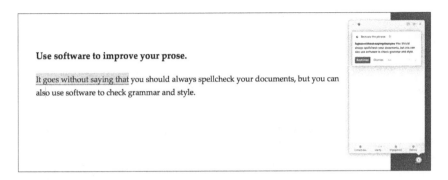

Figure 11.1. Screenshot from Grammarly.

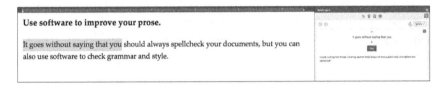

Figure 11.2. Screenshot from BriefCatch.

alternative designed for attorneys is BriefCatch, which hunts for common style and citation errors (figure 11.2). And advances in generative AI technology (such as that underlying OpenAI's ChatGPT software) will soon make tasks like proofreading and citation formatting easier than ever.

These programs supplement but do not replace human editing, and their suggestions should be considered rather than automatically accepted. Editing software not designed for attorneys often incorrectly marks legal text as erroneous and proposes suggestions that would introduce mistakes (for example, suggesting *deposit* as a replacement for *deposition*).

Despite such imperfections, these programs can save writers time when editing and suggest helpful revisions that might otherwise be missed.

11.2. Use dumpfiles to help you revise fearlessly.

Don't become too attached to something you've written in an early draft. Good revision often requires deleting or overhauling text that is well written but ultimately doesn't belong in the final draft.

Two strategies help me overcome any feelings of attachment to my first draft. First, I use *dumpfiles* for writing projects longer than a few pages. A dumpfile is a document in which I paste paragraphs, sentences, or citations that I delete while revising. This makes it psychologically easier to revise, as I can always recover the text from my dumpfile or an earlier draft if I regret deleting it. I sometimes also use the text in my dumpfiles in future projects.

Second, I use *version control* to avoid accidentally losing work. I store my documents in cloud servers so they are always backed up and create copies of files before making significant changes.

11.3. Set up text expansion.

Text expansion programs allow you to type shorthand cues (such as "rbl") and have them automatically expand into full words (such as "reasonable") or even sentences and paragraphs. For example, you could type the text "MSJstandard" and have it expand into a boilerplate legal-standard paragraph for a summary judgment brief.

Although text expansion is built into some operating systems (including Apple's macOS and iOS), I recommend using dedicated software to manage your text snippets. Two good options currently available are the apps aText and PhraseExpress.

In a recent jury trial, I used text expansion and Google Docs to suggest objections to my colleague John Rushing, who was defending cross-examinations of our witnesses. We created a Google Docs document and opened it on my laptop and his tablet, and he brought the tablet to the podium. I set the font size to 24 so he could easily see what I was typing as soon as I typed it. I then set up text-expansion snippets that allowed me to quickly type any standard evidence objection.

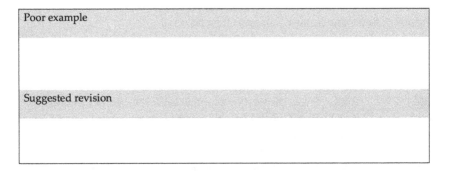

Poor example
Suggested revision

Figure 11.3. Example of an AutoText table in Word.

As an example, suppose the opposing attorney asked our witness: "How do you think Mr. Keller interpreted that statement?" I would type "cs," and my colleague's tablet would display "Calls for speculation." He could then decide whether to make that objection.

Text expansion is also built into Microsoft Word. You may have experienced it unwillingly by typing *(c)* or *(e)*, as in "Rule 15(c)" or "Rule 8(e)," only to have the (c) turn into © or the (e) turn into €.

Any part of a Word document can be turned into an "AutoText" entry that you can replicate with a few keystrokes. Most text expansion systems work with unformatted text, but AutoText entries in Word can preserve the formatting of the original item you copied. When preparing this manuscript, for example, I created an AutoText entry for the table in which I wrote the before-and-after examples. Typing "CompEx" produced the blank table displayed in figure 11.3.

Table 11.1 shows some other text shortcuts from my setup that can give you a sense of what is possible.

11.4. Learn common keyboard shortcuts.

Many computer users rely too much on trackpads and mouse devices instead of keyboards, but constantly moving one's hand between a keyboard and a mouse is inefficient. Many tasks that would require moving a

Table 11.1   Some text-expansion snippets from my setup

Shortcut	Expanded Text
ca4	Cal. App. 4th
cdcal	United States District Court for the Central District of California
crc	Cal. Rules of Court, Rule
emd	— [an em dash]
eml	[My email address]
firmmeeting	[A Zoom URL that my firm uses for its weekly meetings]
frcp	Fed. R. Civ. P.
paras	¶¶
psal	Please see the attached letter.
rbl	reasonable
rmadr	[The address of Rushing McCarl LLP]
sec	§
vscn	["Virgin Scent case number"] *Virgin Scent, Inc. v. BT Supplies W., Inc.* (Case No. 2:21-cv-00184-DMG-AS)
zbd	breach of fiduciary duty
zea	(emphasis added)
zfrcp	Federal Rules of Civil Procedure
zpc	possession, custody, or control
zty	Thank you, Ryan

mouse and clicking several menu items can be performed instantly using a keyboard shortcut.

Keyboard shortcuts are like chords on a piano. They require little technical prowess. At a minimum, everyone should know how to cut, copy, and paste text, and undo and redo changes, using the standard shortcuts listed in table 11.2.

These shortcuts are available in almost all programs that allow you to type text. If you can use them without thinking, then you have a sense of how keyboard shortcuts can save you a lot of time.

It's worth learning the keyboard shortcuts for every command you regularly use in Word and other software—your email and calendar

Table 11.2   Some standard keyboard shortcuts

Action	Windows	Mac
Copy	Ctrl + C	Cmd + C
Cut	Ctrl + X	Cmd + X
Paste	Ctrl + V	Cmd + V
Undo	Ctrl + Z	Cmd + Z
Redo	Ctrl + Y	Shift + Cmd + Z

Table 11.3   Custom shortcuts used in my law firm's templates

Shortcut	Style applied
Ctrl + Shift + Y	Body style
Ctrl + Shift + B	Body Bullets style (create a bulleted list)
Ctrl + Shift + 1	Heading 1 style (create a first-level heading)

programs, internet browser, and so on. Every time you discover a new shortcut that you think you'll use again, write it down on an index card.

You can take this productivity strategy even further in two ways.

First, you can assign new keyboard shortcuts to commands in Word or other software. For example, I created a shortcut in which I open Word's "Customize Keyboard" dialog box by pressing F4; this allows me to quickly create other shortcuts. I've also created shortcuts for applying common formatting styles in my law firm's templates, as shown in table 11.3.

Second, you can assign entire workflows to keyboard shortcuts using software like Keyboard Maestro (Mac) or AutoHotKey (PC). These programs allow you to automate repetitive tasks by creating customized commands called *macros*. For example, I have a "focus on firm work" macro that minimizes all my application windows, then opens my law firm's shared task list, file system, and time-tracking software.

Figure 11.4. Stream Deck, a macro keyboard.

You can assign keyboard shortcuts to macros or buy a macro keyboard such as the Stream Deck (figure 11.4) to trigger them with buttons. It's also possible to run macros and perform other computer tasks by setting up voice commands; in recent years, speech recognition software has dramatically improved, making this method more practical.

11.5. Go beyond the basics with Microsoft Word.

For lawyers, the most important writing software is Microsoft Word. Although the software can be clumsy and frustrating, it is the only word processor suitable for preparing legal documents.

Any time you spend learning to use Word effectively—how to work with and create templates, mark citations, set up tables of contents and tables of authorities, search for and replace text using wildcards,[1] manage lists and outlines, and so on—is time well spent. Watch training videos and go out of your way to try unfamiliar features of the software.

Here are two examples of useful advanced Word features (others, Word's AutoText feature and Styles feature, are discussed in sections 11.3 and 11.6).

Sequence fields

In Microsoft Word, *fields* are snippets of software code that calculate the text to be displayed. The simplest example is a date field. The code { SAVEDATE \@ "MMMM d, yyyy" } appears to the user as the date on which the document was last saved.

Word's automatically generated tables of contents and tables of authorities are also fields. You can see their code by right-clicking them and selecting "Toggle Field Codes."

One useful type of field is a *sequence field*, which is used to create custom numeric sequences. Litigators can use sequence fields to automatically number discovery requests. This allows you to move questions around and add or delete questions without having to manually renumber the list.

Rather than typing "Special Interrogatory No. 5," for example, you would type "Special Interrogatory No." and then insert a space and a sequence field. If you name the sequence of interrogatories "Rog," the text will look like this when the field code is exposed:

Special Interrogatory No. { SEQ Rog }

When the document is printed, that field code will be replaced by a number.

Macros

Macros are bits of software code that allow you to automatize multistep workflows in Word. Anytime you find yourself doing something mindless and repetitive in Word, consider whether you can download or create a macro to do it.[2] Although you can create macros by working directly with software code, Word's "Record Macro" command can write the code for you by observing your keystrokes while the macro is being recorded.

Here are some examples of useful macros:

- Replace every instance of two or more spaces with a single space.
- Replace every space after a § or ¶ sign with a nonbreaking space (preventing unwanted line breaks).
- Replace every hyphen in a numeric range with an en dash.
- Remove a document's metadata (e.g., information about the document's author).
- Delete all comments and remove all tracked changes from the document.

11.6. Use templates and styles to format documents.

Most Microsoft Word users format text manually. If they want to make their text double-spaced, for example, they might select all the text in the document and change its line spacing by clicking a button in the Ribbon. But manual formatting is error-prone and often leads to inconsistencies. Instead, use Word's Styles feature.

Unlike plain-text documents, files created with word processors such as Microsoft Word and Google Docs store both text and formatting information. Each paragraph is linked to a set of formatting rules called a *paragraph style*. In Word, you can see a document's styles by opening the Styles pane from the Home tab of the Ribbon.

I wrote the manuscript of this chapter, for example, using a paragraph style called "Body Text" that includes 12-point font, 1.2× line spacing, and 12 points of blank space after each paragraph (creating block paragraphs).[3] To insert a heading, I clicked "Heading 1" or "Heading 2" in Word's Styles pane (or pressed keyboard shortcuts I've set up for those styles). To italicize text within a paragraph, I didn't click the slanted *I* in the ribbon; instead, I applied a character style called "Italic."

A document's styles are built into its underlying *template*. Most law firms have different templates for letters, court filings, and other purposes. Word's templates may also contain macros, keyboard shortcuts, and preferences.

Table 11.4 shows some paragraph styles built into my default template in Microsoft Word.[4]

Table 11.4 Some paragraph styles in my default Word template

Style name	Style characteristics
Normal	Font: 12 pt. Palatino Linotype, kerned at 8 pt., left-aligned
Body	Settings in Normal, plus 1.2× line spacing and 12 points after each paragraph
Heading Zero	Settings in Body, but center-aligned with bold and small-caps, with "keep lines together" and "keep with next" turned on
Footnote	Settings in Body, but with 11 pt. font, 0.25" hanging indentation, and "keep lines together" turned on (to prevent footnotes from breaking across pages)

Pasting text

To avoid ruining your document's formatting when you paste text, learn about Word's Paste Options menu and how to paste unformatted text. You can find the menu by clicking the drop-down arrow to the right of the clipboard on the Home tab of the Ribbon. When you paste text using this menu's Keep Text Only option, the text will use the paragraph style of the current cursor position without introducing any foreign styles into the document.[5]

11.7. Consider using text editors rather than word processors for early drafts.

Because every paragraph in a Microsoft Word document is linked to information about the text's formatting—its font, spacing, alignment, and so on—Word files are large, and editing them on different systems can cause headaches.

I find formatting options to be a distraction during the early stages of drafting a document. When I'm completing an outline or first draft, I only want to see and think about the text itself. If you have the same concern, one way to force yourself to focus on drafting before formatting is to use a *text editor* (figure 11.5) which removes formatting options other than Markdown.[6]

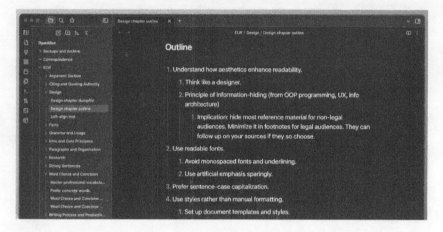

Figure 11.5. An early book outline prepared in Obsidian, a text editor and note organizer.

Plain-text files are small and flexible. They can be read and edited on any platform, with no compatibility problems. Some text editors developed in the 1970s are still popular today.[7]

I use text editors to write first drafts, outlines, lists, sections of documents, and notes. When I got stuck revising this chapter, I pasted it into a folder of text files of about fifteen hundred words each. This helped me focus, made the task feel more manageable, and reminded me to save formatting for later. I could look at my text in small chunks without having to scroll around through a fifty-page document to find my place. Later, after working through each section in a text editor on my tablet, I pasted the text back into my manuscript in Microsoft Word.

Many software programmers use text editors because computer code and webpages are written in plain text. As a result, text editors often have useful features that cannot be found in standard word processors. For example, some programs can search for and replace text across all the files in a computer folder.

12 Document Design

This book began with an announcement of its philosophy: that legal writing should be clear, easy to read, and aesthetically pleasing. The visual appearance of legal documents can further or hinder all three aims, but attorneys rarely give much thought to document design. This chapter will help you craft visually appealing legal documents.

12.1. Be mindful of your documents' appearance and legibility.

The font, spacing, and margin sizes you use won't determine whether you win a motion, but they may impress or repel discerning readers. Formatting choices signal how polished your work is and where your firm sits within the hierarchy of prestige and value in the legal marketplace.

The legal brief pictured in figure 12.1 shows an all-too-common disregard for visual aesthetics, committing the following design errors (departures from generally accepted principles of design and readability):

- The brief is written in Courier New, a font that makes text look as though it were produced by a typewriter. Typewriter-style fonts are less legible and have no place in twenty-first-century legal documents.
- The line numbers in the left margin are bold, violating the design principles of consistency and intentional allocation of emphasis.
- The brief uses two spaces rather than one after periods (another vestige of the typewriter era), which creates what typographers call "rivers" of white space down the page. This practice violates the design principles of keeping alignments clean and using white space intentionally rather than haphazardly.
- The brief uses underlining, a third vestige of the typewriter era. Underlining hampers readability.
- The heading should use sentence case rather than capitalizing the first letter of each word. Text written in ALL CAPS or Initial Caps is harder to read and creates momentary uncertainty about whether the writer is referring to a proper noun.
- The heading should be closer to the left margin. It is floating in no-man's-land about three-quarters of the way across the page.
- The brief should use more white space. The attorney can remove the pointless vertical lines separating the text from the line numbers, add more line spacing before and after the headings, and move the citations to footnotes.

1	*Anderson*, 646 F. Supp. 2d at 1053 (emphasis in original).[23]
2	iv. <u>Derivative Sovereign Immunity</u>
3	Derivative sovereign immunity is not available where plaintiff
4	alleges that a government contractor was negligent. *Cabalce v. VSE*
5	*Corp.*, 922 F. Supp. 2d 1113, 1127 (D. Haw. 2013), *aff'd sub nom.*
6	*Cabalce*, 797 F.3d 720 ("[A]llegations of negligence render the
7	[derivative sovereign immunity] defense inapplicable."). Not even
8	the federal government can claim sovereign immunity for negligence.
9	*Makiri v. United States*, 254 F. App'x 587, 588 (9th Cir. 2007)
10	("The FTCA waives the government's sovereign immunity for tort
11	claims arising out of negligent conduct of government employees
12	acting within the scope of their employment.").

Figure 12.1. A poorly designed legal brief.

12.2. Use footnotes liberally to show the reader what to focus on.

Footnotes have long been disfavored in the legal profession but are increasingly common. Stylists have differing views on how often lawyers should use them and what they should use them for. Some side with tradition and recommend avoiding footnotes entirely,[1] while others argue that they should be used only for reference material.[2]

I disagree with both approaches and see footnotes as essential, especially but not solely for citations. Legal briefs that use footnotes are easier to read.

Footnotes are routinely used in academic and professional writing outside the law. In most fields, writers don't habitually interrupt the reader's flow by putting lengthy citations or other reference material in the main text. Such an intrusion would be unthinkable in a book or magazine.

Although one can find defenses of the anti-footnote view, lawyers' hostility to footnotes is rooted more in tradition than in logic. Modern word processors have made inserting, deleting, and moving footnotes easy, so the question is whether they make briefs easier to read.

The main objection to footnotes is that they remove information from the reader's visual path, requiring them to bounce their focus up and down the page if they wish to read every word. Some readers will opt not to inconvenience themselves in that way, so they may not read the footnotes.

Those arguments would be more compelling if all the information in a brief were equally important and deserving of the reader's focus, but that's not the case. When the judge reads your brief for the first (and perhaps only) time, you want their full attention on your best arguments.

By contrast, you don't want the judge to focus on the reporter volume and page where an unimportant case can be found, a tertiary argument you're making just to avoid waiver, or a rebuttal to an opposing counsel's underhanded assertion that you denied them a professional courtesy. Putting such information in the body of your brief, intermingling it with your narrative and argument, signals that these items are equally important. That's a mistake.

Web designers and programmers are familiar with the principle of *information hiding* (also known as *progressive disclosure*). People solve problems by focusing on information relevant to their current tasks and ignoring everything else; clutter impedes productivity.

If your brief includes an essential detail you want the judge to notice, put it in the main text. Help the reader focus on it by moving unimportant information *out* of the main text. Every brief includes ancillary information that the judge can skip while still following your argument. If you can't delete such information, put it in footnotes.

Footnotes increase visual variety and white space in legal briefs. More importantly, they enhance readability in at least three ways.

First, footnotes allow readers to immediately distinguish essential from secondary information, helping them see what matters most and what they should focus on first.

Second, footnotes allow readers to read a brief straight through, like any other work of prose, without being constantly interrupted by citations they must hurdle to avoid losing track of the author's point. Unlike in-text citations or digressions spanning several lines of text, footnote references are easily ignored. The reader can always visit the footnote if they wish to check a source or learn more about the topic being discussed.

Third, footnotes help readers find information when they need it and ignore it when they don't. At times, an appellate brief makes an eyebrow-raising assertion about something that occurred at trial, and the judge may wish to check the record. If the brief uses footnotes, the judge need only trace the footnote reference to the bottom of the page to find the record citation. If the brief doesn't use footnotes, the judge will find the citation in the body text—along with dozens of other citations the judge doesn't need, each of which is an unsightly distraction.

Contrast the examples below. The first places record citations in the main text, as is traditional; the second relegates bibliographic information to footnotes. Note how the citations in the first example create visual disorder, interrupting the reader's flow:

In June 2004, when Baxter was copied on an internal routing form enclosing the cover letters and expense reports from ACHA for half of 2002 and CY2003, A699 (GX-0319), he forwarded them to the lawyers, Briggs and Clarke, A699 (GX-0315a). Briggs promptly responded that "our team [i.e.,

CareWell's legal team] has been activated on the BH expenditures." A700
(D_1558).

Suggested revision (replacing the record citations with footnote
references):

> In June 2004, when Baxter was copied on an internal routing form enclos-
> ing the cover letters and expense reports from ACHA for half of 2002 and
> CY2003,[1] he forwarded them to the lawyers, Briggs and Clarke.[2] Briggs
> promptly responded that "our team [i.e., CareWell's legal team] has been
> activated on the BH expenditures."[3]

The guidelines that follow will help you use footnotes effectively.

Reserve the document's body text for information that is essential to
the argument or otherwise deserving of the reader's focus when they first
read your brief from start to finish. Almost everything else can be deleted
or put in footnotes.

Use footnotes whenever the material in the footnote might interrupt
the reader for no good reason, distract the reader from your argument, or
show the reader information they don't need to think about when they
first read your brief.

Always put these in footnotes:

- Citations to filings, appellate records, and deposition and trial
  transcripts.
- Bibliographic reference material, such as a case's reporter volume and
  page number, that will be needed only if readers look up the cited source
  for themselves.

Consider putting some or all of these in footnotes, too:

- Citations to sources you don't discuss in the body text, especially
  citations supporting familiar and undisputed legal rules.
- Citations that directly support a legal rule, with no explanation or
  analogies needed.
- Minor substantive points that depart from the main argument,
  including arguments you're raising just to avoid waiver and responses to
  an opponent's insignificant contentions.

In most briefs, only a handful of cases are important enough to warrant discussion in the body text. Even then, put the case's name in the body text while putting reference information in a footnote, as in this example:

> It makes no difference whether Hunt's purported assignment to Rose was a contractual offer or an attempted grant; both offers and grants must be accepted to have any effect. As the California Court of Appeals explained in *Richardson v. Abernathy*, grants fail if they are delivered by the grantor but not accepted by the grantee.[1] The assignment was extinguished when Rose rejected it, so title never transferred. Hunt alone owns the property.
>
> [1] *See* 23 Cal. App. 2d 629, 631–32 (1937).

Don't use footnotes as junk drawers, though. Every substantive footnote in a legal brief is suspect, because its information wasn't important enough to be put in the body text yet the writer included it anyway. As always, be concise and delete information that doesn't help the reader.

12.3. Use legible fonts.

Some fonts are more legible and suitable for legal work than others.[3] Ideal fonts for legal documents are like those used in novels or works of general nonfiction: neutral and professional, drawing little attention to themselves and allowing for comfortable extended reading. I recommend Palatino Linotype or Century Schoolbook.

Proportional vs. monospaced fonts

Legal documents should use proportionally spaced fonts, which adjust the horizontal space used by each letter to the letter's shape. Legal documents should avoid Courier and other monospaced fonts designed to look like they were produced by typewriters. Typewriters use monospaced fonts because the hammer strikes the page with the same width each time; no such limitation applies to computer printers.

Serif vs. sans serif fonts

Some fonts have *serifs*, little notches at the edges of certain letters (e.g., "M"). Legal documents should use serif fonts; sans serif fonts are best reserved for digital and informal settings.

Recommended fonts

To maximize legibility, use one of these proportionally spaced, serif fonts in legal documents:[4]

Book Antiqua

Century Schoolbook

Palatino Linotype

One difference to notice among these fonts is the way they seem to vary in size. A font's *x-height* is the height of the lowercase letters if you ignore their *ascenders* (such as the vertical line that begins a lowercase *b*) and *descenders* (such as the vertical line that begins a lowercase *p*). Fonts with larger x-heights appear larger than other fonts using the same point size, so they tend to be more legible.

Fonts to avoid

Avoid sans serif and monospaced fonts, especially these common fonts, no matter how many attorneys use them:

Arial

Calibri

Courier New

Times New Roman

Verdana

Many jurisdictions' court rules include language suggesting or mandating Times New Roman, which is unusually narrow, just as they sometimes require narrow margins, line numbers, and double spacing. Check the rules' exact language to see whether they allow any discretion on these points. A few courts—notably the U.S. Court of Appeals for the Seventh

Circuit and the U.S. Supreme Court—have rules that are more aligned with sound typography practices.[5]

12.4. Design attractive headings.

A brief's headings are often the first thing a reader looks for. Their design should be more than an afterthought.

The heading in figure 12.2 is illegible because it cramps together single-spaced lines of all-caps text that is both bold and underlined. Follow these guidelines to write well-formatted point headings:

- Use sentence-case capitalization.
- Limit each heading to three or four lines of text.
- Don't allow page breaks to interrupt the heading or separate it from the text that follows.
- Use a standard outline format with up to four levels. For contracts, use a pure decimal-numbering system, such as 1, 1.1, 1.1.1, 1.1.1.1; or a modified version, such as 1, 1.1, 1.1(A), 1.1(A)(1), 1.1(A)(1)(a). For legal briefs, use a similar decimal system or one of the traditional outline formats: either I, A, 1, a, or I, A, (1), (a).[6]
- Use hanging indents so that the text on each line is aligned.
- Surround each heading with at least 12 points of vertical white space above and below the text. The heading should be either equidistant between the surrounding paragraphs or closer to the next paragraph than to the preceding paragraph.

The last two items may require elaboration. *Hanging indents* are used in numbered and bulleted lists, footnotes, and outlines to indent the text after the number or bullet but keep the text aligned if it runs to more than one line. These are implemented correctly in figure 12.2: notice how the second line's text aligns with the first line's text.

12.5. Avoid unnecessary capitalization.

Resist the lawyerly habit of writing headings in all-caps or initial-caps styles rather than sentence case. Use standard sentence-case capitalization whenever you can.

17	
18	**I.** <u>**THIS COURT MUST CONSIDER DOCUMENTS NOT ATTACHED TO**</u>
	<u>**THE COMPLAINT ON A MOTION TO DISMISS IF THEY ARE**</u>
	<u>**INCORPORATED BY REFERENCE IN THE COMPLAINT OR**</u>
19	<u>**PROPERLY THE SUBJECT OF JUDICIAL NOTICE.**</u>
20	When ruling on a motion to dismiss pursuant to 12(b)(6) of the Federal Rules of
21	Civil Procedure, a court must consider "documents incorporated into the complaint by
22	reference, and matters of which a court may take judicial notice." *Tellabs, Inc. v.*
23	*Makor Issues & Rights, Ltd.*, 127 S. Ct. 2499, 2509 (2007); *Metzler Inv. GMBH v.*
24	*Corinthian Colls., Inc.*, No. 06-55826, 2008 WL 3905427, at *8 (9th Cir. Aug. 26,
25	2008). Thus, there are two independent bases for considering information outside the
26	complaint: (1) documents incorporated by reference into the complaint, and (2) facts
27	that are properly the subject of judicial notice pursuant to Federal Rule of Evidence
28	201.

Figure 12.2. Poor heading design in a legal brief.

There is no excuse for writing in all-caps, whether out of habit or to create emphasis. All-caps sentences are harder to read because they disguise the shapes of words. Also, in the internet era, many people interpret all-caps writing as signifying shouting. You wouldn't shout in a courtroom, so don't shout in your briefs or emails.

I recommend using title case rather than initial caps for document titles, labels, and defined terms. Consider using small-caps formatting along with title case for titles at the top of briefs (e.g., "MEMORANDUM OF POINTS AND AUTHORITIES") and unnumbered zero-level point headings (e.g., "CORPORATE DISCLOSURE STATEMENT"). If you're tempted to use all-caps, use small-caps instead.

12.6. Use artificial emphasis sparingly.

Attorneys commonly try to strengthen their points by underlining them, bolding them, italicizing them, or doing several of these at once, as in the brief pictured in figure 12.3. Artificial emphasis must be used sparingly to be effective—up to once or twice per document. Anything more will cause

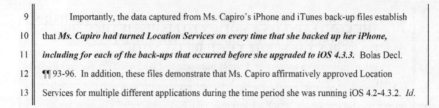

9	Importantly, the data captured from Ms. Capiro's iPhone and iTunes back-up files establish
10	that *Ms. Capiro had turned Location Services on every time that she backed up her iPhone,*
11	*including for each of the back-ups that occurred before she upgraded to iOS 4.3.3.* Bolas Decl.
12	¶¶ 93-96. In addition, these files demonstrate that Ms. Capiro affirmatively approved Location
13	Services for multiple different applications during the time period she was running iOS 4.2-4.3.2. *Id.*

Figure 12.3. Excessive artificial emphasis.

it to lose its effect and may make the document's tone seem overwrought or unprofessional.[7]

Although underlining is never recommended, and boldface should be reserved mostly for point headings, you can sometimes use italics to emphasize text or introduce unfamiliar words. You can also italicize a word or phrase to make it less likely that the reader misreads the sentence or overlooks a key point. Here's a good example from a brief that uses italics to emphasize a fact distinguishing an opponent's citation:

> Hart cites no authority suggesting that filing a lawsuit can constitute anticipatory repudiation. He relies only on a century-old case in which a party repudiated a contract *before any suit was filed.*[1] The case does not support Hart's claim that filing a lawsuit can constitute anticipatory repudiation.
>
> [1] *See Passow & Sons v. Harris,* 29 Cal. App. 559, 562–63 (1916).

12.7. Use lots of white space.

Most well-designed documents use simple designs with expansive white space. Besides making it easier to focus on and process text, white space encourages readers to keep reading. Dense pages and long blocks of unbroken text are daunting. Readers instinctively turn away from documents that seem to promise a slog.

Use the layout and text design guidelines below to present your document in manageable, inviting visual chunks.

Page-layout guidelines

Wider margins. Well-formatted legal documents use larger margins, which make text easier to read by reducing the length of lines. Depending on the document and any applicable court rules, acceptable margin sizes range from 1.0 to 2.5 inches on each side. The bottom margin may be made slightly larger than the top margin.[8]

Clean margins without vertical lines. Legal filings often use line numbers that are separated from the body text by one or two vertical lines. Some attorneys also include vertical lines to the right of the body, boxing it in on two sides. These lines serve no purpose and duplicate the role played by the text's margins. Unless court rules require you to do otherwise, ditch the vertical lines, line numbers, or both in favor of white space.[9]

Simple headers and footers. Keep headers and footers mostly empty except for page numbers. In the footer of legal filings, write a one-line shorthand description of the filing rather than the filing's full name.

No marketing. Avoid putting your law firm's name or address in legal filings' headers, footers, or margins. Readers can find that information on the cover.

Text-design guidelines

Headings and subheadings. Err on the side of using more rather than fewer headings. But ensure that there are at least two sub-items for each level of an outline or list. For example, every bulleted or numbered list must have at least two items. Every heading in an outline must have either no subheadings or at least two subheadings (never just one).

Bulleted or numbered lists. Lists are an easy way to create visual variety and show the reader how information is organized. Mid-sentence lists whose items are separated by numbers in closed parentheses—(1), (2), and so on—are also helpful for tasks such as listing the elements of a claim.

Visuals, diagrams, and tables. Visual aids can help the reader understand your brief while making it more interesting.

Shorter paragraphs. Enormous paragraphs often go unread, so err on the side of using more paragraph breaks while ensuring that each paragraph is unified and has a topic sentence.

Example

Many contracts are printed in cramped, single-spaced fine print. Figure 12.4 shows a more thoughtfully designed contract—notice its generous

Operating Agreement of Acme LLC

This limited liability company operating agreement ("Agreement") of
Acme LLC (the "Company") is entered into as of November 23, 2021,
between Acme LLC and the persons and entities listed on Schedule A (the
"Members").

Recitals

1. → On or before November 23, 2021, Articles of Organization for the
Company, a California limited liability company, were filed with
the California Secretary of State.

2. → The Members wish to adopt and approve an operating agreement
for the Company under the California Limited Liability Company
Act.

1. → **Definitions**

1.1. → "Contribution" means a monetary benefit provided by a
Member to the Company as capital.

1.2. → "Distributable Cash" means the portion of the cash in the
Company's bank accounts that is available for distribution to
the Members after a reasonable provision has been made for
cash reserves.

1.3. → "Member" means any person or entity admitted to the
Company as a member in accordance with this Agreement. The
Members of the Company and their respective membership
percentages are reflected on Schedule A, which may be
amended.

1 of 9

Figure 12.4. A well-formatted contract (as displayed in Microsoft Word).

use of white space through wide margins (1 inch on the top, 2 inches on
the bottom, 1.5 inches on the sides) as well as 1.2× spacing, with additional space around the headings.

1
2
3
4
5
6
7
8
9
10
11
12
13
14
15
16
17
18

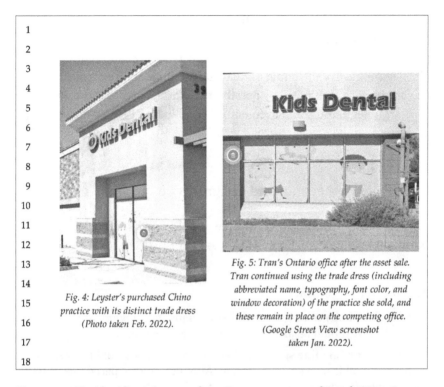

Fig. 4: Leyster's purchased Chino practice with its distinct trade dress (Photo taken Feb. 2022).

Fig. 5: Tran's Ontario office after the asset sale. Tran continued using the trade dress (including abbreviated name, typography, font color, and window decoration) of the practice she sold, and these remain in place on the competing office. (Google Street View screenshot taken Jan. 2022).

Figure 12.5. Visual evidence in a complaint. Imagery courtesy of Google Maps Street View.

12.8. Use images, tables, text boxes, and other visual aids.

The most eye-catching legal documents often use well-designed images, flowcharts, diagrams, or tables to tell a story or help the reader understand a complex idea or abstract data.

The complaint pictured in figure 12.5 used a side-by-side comparison to show similarities between the branding of two dentists' offices. This tactic brought relevant evidence to the court's attention at the earliest opportunity while delaying arguments about whether the evidence was admissible.

Look for opportunities to strategically bend the formal norms of legal filings to benefit your client while helping the reader. Graphics sometimes allow lawyers to dramatize abstract disputes while making filings more interesting and easier to read.

Putting screenshots of evidence in your pleadings and motions is just the beginning. Try including an "Executive Summary" text box at the top of your brief to eliminate any possibility that the judge will overlook your best argument. You could even embed a video in a PDF or include a QR code inviting the reader to visit a website.

12.9. Follow other standard design advice.

Attorneys can make documents more visually appealing by following the additional design guidelines listed below.

Spacing and alignment

Left-align body text. Use left rather than justified alignment for body text.[10] Text should be justified only in block quotations.

Use 1.2× or 1.5× line spacing. There is a reason books and magazines do not use double or even 1.5× spacing. Although single-spaced lines are too narrow, excessive line spacing makes text harder to read. In documents other than court filings, I recommend 1.2× line spacing. In court filings, I recommend 1.5× line spacing.[11]

Delete excess spaces. Use one space rather than two after sentence-ending punctuation. Avoid having leading or trailing spaces at the beginning or end of a line or paragraph.

Create manual page breaks. Most attorneys allow their word processors to decide where to end one page and start the next. But this often leads to visually awkward results, such as an argument section that begins at the bottom of a page. When that happens, consider overriding the software by inserting a page break before the heading.[12]

Use nonbreaking spaces to prevent awkward line breaks. Using a *nonbreaking space* (aka *hard space*) prevents line breaks at the space's location. This too prevents visually awkward results, such as having a line end with a section (§) or paragraph (¶) symbol. Create a keyboard shortcut (such as Ctrl + Shift + Space) to insert nonbreaking spaces quickly.

Indentation

Use hanging indents. Use hanging indents for bulleted lists, numbered lists, outlines, and footnotes.

Avoid the Tab key. Use Word's formatting styles to set indentation rules.

Punctuation

Use curved quotation marks. Unless you're writing computer code, use curved (aka "smart") quotation marks (" ") and apostrophes ('), not straight ones (' and "). Use prime symbols (′ and ″) only for measurements.

Use en dashes. In numeric ranges, use an en dash (–) rather than a hyphen (-).

Use em dashes. Do not use a double hyphen (--) to replace an em dash (—).

Notes

Chapter 1. Core Principles of Legal Writing

1. For more on the ideas discussed in this section, see Carol S. Dweck, *Mindset: The New Psychology of Success* (Random House 2006).

2. See K. Anders Ericsson et al., *The Role of Deliberate Practice in the Acquisition of Expert Performance*, 100 Psych. Rev. 363, 367 (1993).

3. The concept of readability draws on ideas from cognitive psychology (information processing), psycholinguistics, composition, rhetoric, information architecture, and design.

4. See Matthew Butterick, *Typography for Lawyers: Essential Tools for Polished & Persuasive Documents* 41–44 (Jones-McClure 2013).

5. I use footnotes routinely in litigation briefs to keep the body text clear of bibliographic references and departures from the argument's main thread. My approach to footnotes is explained in section 12.2.

6. See E. D. Hirsch Jr., *The Philosophy of Composition* 7 (Univ. Chicago Press 1977). Hirsch argues that writers should make their writing "self-contextual." *Id.* at 8.

7. A related tip for law students is to avoid "outline dumps" on law exams. Don't try to cram as much of your outline as possible into an answer to show how much you've learned. Professors evaluate your legal analysis and judgment, not your skills as a notetaker.

Chapter 2. Concision

1. Recognizing and replacing suboptimal words and language patterns is, along with citation formatting, the legal-writing task most easily automated with software.

2. See Antonin Scalia & Bryan A. Garner, *Reading Law: The Interpretation of Legal Texts* 199–213 (West 2012).

3. See *Yates v. United States*, 574 U.S. 528 (2015).

4. For a thorough list of legal doublets and triplets, see Bryan A. Garner, *The Redbook: A Manual on Legal Style* § 12.2 (West 4th ed. 2018).

5. See also the discussion of buried verbs in section 4.5. For many more condensable phrases and phrase structures, see Robert Hartwell Fiske, *To the Point: A Dictionary of Concise Writing* (W. W. Norton 2014).

Chapter 3. Plain Language

1. See Anthony Esgate & David Groome et al., *An Introduction to Applied Cognitive Psychology* 12–24 (Psych. Press 2004).

2. Hirsch describes this as "semantic closure." Semantic closure occurs when we make a final decision about what a clause means or refers to. See E. D. Hirsch Jr., *The Philosophy of Composition* 108–19 (Univ. Chicago Press 1977). Many of my discussions of readability draw on concepts I encountered in Hirsch's book.

3. For a useful discussion gathering some of these guidelines into one place, see Bruce Ross-Larson, *Edit Yourself: A Manual for Everyone Who Works with Words* 9–12 (Barnes & Noble 1996).

4. Jacques Barzun, *Simple & Direct: A Rhetoric for Writers* 113 (Harper Collins 4th ed. 2001) (discussing what Barzun calls the "pseudo-technical tone").

5. Some stylists—notably Strunk and White—disparage *contact* as an example of jargon. See William Strunk Jr. & E. B. White, *The Elements of Style Illustrated* 68 (Penguin 2007). If you know how the communication occurred, use a more specific verb, such as *called* or *emailed*. But *contact* is a fine word choice if the method of communication is unknown or unimportant.

6. The verb *shall* is, properly used, a term of art in legal drafting that means "has a duty to." It creates a promise or duty. See Tina L. Stark, *Drafting Contracts: How and Why Lawyers Do What They Do* 126–27 (Wolters Kluwer 2007). Even so, Garner recommends avoiding it. See Bryan A. Garner, *A Dictionary of Modern Legal Usage* 939–40 (Oxford Univ. Press 2d ed. 1995).

7. See Garner, *supra* note 6, at 631 (endorsing *overparticularization* as a useful term to describe attorneys' habitual inclusion of irrelevant details).

8. A statement is *conclusory* if it asserts a disputable legal conclusion without supporting that conclusion with the necessary facts, law, and reasoning. Conclusory reasoning is discussed in section 7.4.

9. Definitions: *alter ego* ("another I") = an entity whose separate corporate status should be disregarded because its owners have not treated it as separate from themselves; *ex parte* ("from one party") = when one party seeks relief from a court without the other party being present; *guardian ad litem* ("guardian for the proceeding") = in family law, an appointed representative of someone who lacks capacity; *habeas corpus* ("you have the body") = a petition asking a court to release someone from custody; *in pari delicto* ("in equal fault") = an affirmative defense contending that the plaintiff's claim is barred because they are equally at fault; *inter vivos* ("between living persons") = in property and estate law, a gift between living persons; *pari passu* ("on equal footing" or "without preference") = in debt law, a bond clause providing that if the borrower makes payments to other creditors, the borrower must also make pro rata payments to the creditor who issued the bond; *ultra vires* ("beyond the power") = an act that exceeds the actor's authority.

10. See Bryan A. Garner, *Garner's Modern English Usage* 215–16 (Oxford Univ. Press 2016).

11. See Nina Totenberg, *Justice Scalia: Be Likeable and Avoid Contractions*, NPR.org (Apr. 28, 2008), www.npr.org/2008/04/28/90001031/justice-scalia-be-likeable-and-avoid-contractions (visited Feb. 7, 2023).

12. Rudolf Flesch, *The Art of Readable Writing* 97 (Collier 1967), quoted in Garner, *supra* note 10, at 216 (italics in original).

Chapter 4. Strong Sentences

1. Jacques Barzun, *Simple & Direct: A Rhetoric for Writers* 58 (HarperCollins 4th ed. 2001).

2. Note the uncertainty created by this sentence's use of the passive voice. Whose residence is being referred to in the phrase "her residence"?

3. Joseph M. Williams, *Style: Toward Clarity and Grace* 21–23 (Univ. Chicago Press 1990).

4. See Noah A. Messing, *The Art of Advocacy: Briefs, Motions, and Writing Strategies of America's Best Lawyers* 279–85 (Wolters Kluwer 2013) (listing two thousand short verbs that can enliven prose).

5. See Bryan A. Garner, *The Winning Brief: 100 Tips for Persuasive Briefing in Trial and Appellate Courts* 165–66 (Oxford Univ. Press 1999).

6. A *subordinate clause* (also known as a *dependent clause*) contains a subject and verb but cannot stand alone as a sentence. Subordinate clauses must be linked to an independent clause.

7. To find illogical statements when you revise, briefly adopt a pedantic and uncooperative attitude toward your own writing. Think about how a fault-finding reader (such as opposing counsel) might interpret your sentence.

8. Although the serial-comma rule is often described as up for debate, with valid opinions on both sides, I have yet to find a legal-writing expert who advocates omitting such commas. They are often essential for avoiding ambiguity.

9. For more on sentence structures, see Virginia Tufte, *Artful Sentences: Syntax as Style* (Graphics Press 2006); June Casagrande, *It Was the Best of Sentences, It Was the Worst of Sentences: A Writer's Guide to Crafting Killer Sentences* (Crown 2010); Brooks Landon, *Building Great Sentences: How to Write the Kind of Sentences You Love to Read* (Plume 2013); and Ann Longknife & K. D. Sullivan, *The Art of Styling Sentences* (Barron's 5th ed. 2012).

10. An *appositive* is a noun phrase that describes an immediately preceding noun phrase, as in "The plaintiff, *a vexatious litigant*, has been repeatedly sanctioned by the courts for his frivolous filings." A *relative clause* is a clause that follows and modifies a noun phrase, as in "The judge scolded the attorney *who showed up late*."

11. Richard A. Lanham, *Revising Prose* 40–44 (Scribner's 1979).

12. See Joe Glaser, *Understanding Style: Practical Ways to Improve Your Writing* 162 (Oxford Univ. Press 1979).

Chapter 5. Organization and Cohesion

1. See Kenneth L. Higbee, *Your Memory: How It Works and How to Improve It* 19 (Prentice Hall 2d ed. 1988); George A. Miller, *The Magical Number Seven, Plus or Minus Two: Some Limits on Our Capacity for Processing Information*, 63 Psych. Rev. 81 (1956); Nelson Cowan, *The Magical Number 4 in Short-Term Memory: A Reconsideration of Mental Storage Capacity*, 24 Behavioral & Brain Sci. 87 (2001).

2. Ross Guberman identified a similar technique in which expert litigators often distinguish lines of cases all at once, a move he labeled "one fell swoop." See Ross Guberman, *Point Made: How to Write Like the Nation's Top Advocates* 149–86 (Oxford Univ. Press 2d ed. 2014).

3. Transitions are an example of *cohesive ties*, a term referring to any device that connects and unifies a text. See M. A. K. Halliday & Ruqaiya Hasan, *Cohesion in English* 3–4 (Longman 2d ed. 1977). For an accessible overview of cohesion, see Martha Kolln & Loretta Gray, *Rhetorical Grammar: Grammatical Choices, Rhetorical Effects* 84–104 (Pearson 6th ed. 2010).

4. For a more extensive list, see Guberman, *supra* note 2, at 274–78.

5. Richard Lanham, *Revising Prose* 54 (Scribner's 1979).

Chapter 6. Tone and Professionalism

1. See Fed. R. Civ. P. 11.

2. In the parable of the good Samaritan (Luke 10:29–35), Jesus said: "A man was going down from Jerusalem to Jericho, when he was attacked by robbers. They stripped him of his clothes, beat him and went away, leaving him half dead." Was it appropriate to call the other side the "thieves" of the parable?

3. Steven D. Stark, *Writing to Win: The Legal Writer* 187 (Crown 2012) (quoting Shakespeare).

Chapter 7. Briefs and Motions

1. Dicta in Supreme Court cases are sometimes treated as binding on lower courts. See, e.g., *Cuevas v. United States*, 778 F.3d 267, 272–73 (1st Cir. 2015).

2. In a brief I have used as an example in my courses, an attorney used 368 words and nine citations to describe the Rule 12(b)(6) standard for motions to dismiss.

Chapter 8. Using Legal Authority

1. The snippet of dialogue is from *Apollo 13* (MCA Universal Home Video 1995), dir. Ron Howard. You can find clips of the scene online.

2. The canonical example of a landmark treatise is Charles A. Wright and Arthur R. Miller's *Federal Practice and Procedure*. Other persuasive secondary sources include model statutes, such as the Restatement (Second) of Torts, and their accompanying commentary.

3. Maxims of equity are general legal principles, such as "[One] who consents to an act is not wronged by it." Cal. Civ. Code § 3515.

4. This argument structure appears in the first example of section 8.6 (an excerpt from a brief written by attorneys for Google).

5. Each parenthetical begins with the present participle *holding*, ensuring that all are grammatically parallel.

6. Opponents sometimes miss the point of such citations and protest that the cited case is not analogous. Your argument may need to show why a rule applies to your case, but not every case you cite as backing for the rule needs to be analogous.

7. Also note the example's effective use of hyphenated compound adjectives to compress information and create parallelism: "bank-fraud statute," "healthcare-fraud statute."

8. See Carolyn V. Williams, *ALWD Guide to Legal Citation* (Wolters Kluwer 7th ed. 2021).

9. Paraphrases should be neutral descriptions of the paraphrased text, without including debatable characterizations or interpretations. Relatedly, it's usually inappropriate to paraphrase an opponent's statement.

10. See Theodore (Jack) Metzler, *Cleaning Up Quotations*, 18 J. App. Prac. & Process 143 (2017).

11. Note that when you delete material at the beginning of a quotation, you don't use an ellipsis. If needed, use an alteration to capitalize the first letter of the quotation.

Chapter 9. Legal Storytelling

1. I single out plaintiffs' attorneys because defendants often have an interest in keeping litigation boring rather than visceral. Crafting narratives is equally important for defense attorneys, though. If an injury has occurred, a jury may expect an explanation of who is responsible.

2. The key word is *subtly*. Overt emotional appeals are improper and unpersuasive in litigation. Legal arguments likewise don't belong in fact sections. Nor do modifiers and characterizations (e.g., "Plaintiff was driving at an unsafe speed") or legal conclusions (e.g., "Plaintiff was driving to the store within the scope of her employment when . . ."). Just say what happened and persuade through your selection and arrangement of the available facts.

3. A fact is *relevant* if it can properly be considered in applying a relevant legal rule. A fact is *material* if it can, either by itself or in tandem with other facts, determine whether a legal test is satisfied.

4. 549 U.S. 346 (2007). Citations are omitted from the brief excerpts.

5. Every fact mentioned in an appellate brief must include a citation to the record, but record citations have no place in the *body text* of a brief, where you're trying to hold the reader's interest and tell a compelling story. They belong in footnotes, as discussed in Section 12.2.

Chapter 10. The Mental Game of Writing

1. It may help to take a break by switching to another task before revisiting the problem later.

2. See Mary Barnard Ray & Barbara J. Cox, *Beyond the Basics: A Text for Advanced Legal Writing* 8–21 (West 2d ed. 2003).

3. The "next action" idea is central to David Allen's popular Getting Things Done (GTD) productivity system. See David Allen, *Getting Things Done: The Art of Stress-Free Productivity* (Penguin 2002).

4. The startup-culture concept of a "minimum viable product" (MVP) is relevant to litigation filings. Every litigation filing has a minimum bar below which the document is too incomplete or poorly executed to be filed. Because of the paramount importance of filing litigation documents on time and avoiding serious mistakes such as accidentally waiving a client's rights, it is sometimes advisable to prepare superficially finished and minimally acceptable documents early in the drafting process, with the idea that you have something you can file in an emergency if you run out of time.

5. See Mayo Clinic, *Office Ergonomics: Your How-To Guide* (Apr. 27, 2019), www.mayoclinic.org/healthy-lifestyle/adult-health/in-depth/office-ergonomics /art-20046169 (visited Jan. 1, 2023).

6. See Mihaly Csikszentmihalyi, *Flow: The Psychology of Optimal Experience* (HarperCollins 1991).

7. For more suggestions on getting sustained intellectual work done despite the distractions of modern technology, see Cal Newport, *Deep Work: Rules for Focused Success in a Distracted World* (Grand Central 2016). See also Nicholas Carr, *The Shallows: What the Internet Is Doing to Our Brains* (W. W. Norton 2020).

8. See Bryan A. Garner, *Legal Writing in Plain English* 9–10 (Univ. Chicago Press 2d ed. 2013); Betty S. Flowers, *Madman, Architect, Carpenter, Judge: Roles and the Writing Process*, www.ut-ie.com/b/b_flowers.html (visited Jan. 16, 2023).

9. Jack Kerouac famously wrote *On the Road* in a three-week drug-fueled bender, typewriting it on a 120-foot scroll without paragraph breaks. See Andrea Shea, *Jack Kerouac's Famous Scroll, 'On the Road' Again*, NPR.org (July 5, 2007).

10. Anne Lamott, *Bird by Bird: Some Instructions on Writing and Life* 21–27 (Knopf 2007).

11. For more helpful editing tips, see Stephen V. Armstrong & Timothy P. Terrell, *Thinking Like a Writer: A Lawyer's Guide to Effective Writing and Editing* 309–30 (Practising Law Institute 3d ed. 2009).

12. For word usage, refer to Bryan A. Garner, *Garner's Modern English Usage* (Oxford Univ. Press 2016), and a good dictionary. For citation formatting, use Carolyn V. Williams, *ALWD Guide to Legal Citation* (Wolters Kluwer 7th ed. 2021); for style, Bryan A. Garner, *The Redbook: A Manual on Legal Style* (West 4th ed. 2018); and for grammar, Mark Lester & Larry Beason, *The McGraw-Hill Education Handbook of English Grammar and Usage* (McGraw-Hill Education 3d ed. 2018).

13. You can also use text-to-speech apps to listen to briefs, treatise chapters, and other texts while you walk around or do the dishes.

Chapter 11. Writing with Technology

1. Wildcards are symbols that allow advanced and inexact text searches. In Lexis, for example, the search query *partne! /p agen!* would look for paragraphs in which a word like *partner* or *partnership* appears in the same paragraph as a word like *agent* or *agency*.

2. Microsoft Word macros can contain viruses, so use macros only from trusted sources.

3. Microsoft Word has both paragraph and character styles. Paragraph styles apply to entire "paragraphs," which Word considers to be any line of text that is followed by a paragraph break. Pressing "Enter" or "Return" on your keyboard creates a paragraph break.

4. The default template in Word is called "Normal," and it's stored in a file called "Normal.dotm." I use separate templates for letters, briefs, and contracts. See chapter 12 for document design guidelines.

5. I recommend setting up a keyboard shortcut to paste unformatted text. Find the PasteTextOnly command on Word's Customize Keyboard menu and set up a shortcut such as Ctrl + Shift + V.

6. Markdown is a flexible, easy-to-learn formatting system for text documents. As an example, you use # symbols to create headings, and asterisks to indicate italics or bold. Markdown programs can then display these text-only documents with formatting as though they had been created in a word processor. You can learn and experiment with Markdown online.

7. These include Emacs and Vi, both first released in 1976.

Chapter 12. Document Design

1. See Tom Goldstein & Jethro K. Lieberman, *The Lawyer's Guide to Writing Well* 110 (Univ. Cal. Press 3d ed. 2016) (calling footnotes the "biggest interruption to the reader's train of thought"). For a practitioner's defense of the anti-footnote tradition, see Peter M. Mansfield, *Citational Footnotes: Should Garner Win the Battle Against the In-Line Tradition?*, 19 Appalachian J.L. 163 (2020).

2. Bryan Garner, for example, advocates putting citations in footnotes but argues that footnotes should not contain any substantive information. See Bryan A. Garner, *The Winning Brief: 100 Tips for Persuasive Briefing in Trial and Appellate Courts* 114 (Oxford Univ. Press 1999).

3. Typographers refer to type designs as *typefaces*. I use the more common term *font*, ignoring its technical meaning.

4. Other good fonts include Century, Palatino, Baskerville, and Garamond.

5. I first learned about the importance of typography from Judge Frank H. Easterbrook of the United States Court of Appeals for the Seventh Circuit, whose

Legal Interpretation course I had the privilege of taking at the University of Chicago Law School. The Seventh Circuit publishes a document called Requirements and Suggestions for Typography in Briefs and Other Papers. See https://www.ca7.uscourts.gov/forms/type.pdf (visited Feb. 5, 2023).

6. For varying perspectives on numbering multilevel lists, see Bryan A. Garner, *The Redbook: A Manual of Legal Style* § 4.21 (West 4th ed. 2018); Matthew Butterick, *Typography for Lawyers: Essential Tools for Polished & Persuasive Documents* 106–07 (Jones McClure 2013); and Tina L. Stark, *Drafting Contracts: How and Why Lawyers Do What They Do* 220–22 (Aspen 2007).

7. Note that italics are already ubiquitous in legal writing because of legal citation style, which italicizes citation signals and case names. This practice makes italics less effective for conveying emphasis.

8. When the top and bottom margins are equally sized, the text can appear to sag on the page. See Butterick, *supra* note 6, at 144.

9. See Butterick, *supra* note 6, at 204.

10. One designer explains that left-aligned (or "flush-left, rag-right") text is helpful for long passages because consistent spacing between words increases legibility, and "the eye of the reader can return to an easy-to-locate place when beginning every line of text." Ina Saltz, *Typography Essentials: 100 Design Principles for Working with Type* 178 (Rockport 2009).

11. If the court's rules mandate double spacing, set the spacing to exactly double the text size (e.g., exactly 24 points of line spacing for 12-point text). See Butterick, *supra* note 6, at 140.

12. The default keyboard shortcut for a page break is Ctrl + Enter (Cmd + Enter on a Mac).

Other Resources

Visit www.elegantlegalwriting.com to sign up for my email newsletter, see my latest recommendations for writing technology, and explore other resources about legal writing.

Most examples in this book are adapted from legal filings found in online databases. I've changed names to protect the litigants' and attorneys' privacy and adjusted the excerpts as needed for reasons of space and pedagogy.

Here are some writing-related books I've consulted in recent years that have influenced my views on craft. Others are mentioned in the notes.

Kenneth A. Adams, *A Manual of Style for Contract Drafting* (ABA 5th ed. 2023)

Stephen V. Armstrong & Timothy P. Terrell, *Thinking Like a Writer: A Lawyer's Guide to Effective Writing and Editing* (Practising Law Institute 3d ed. 2009)

Jacques Barzun, *Simple & Direct: A Rhetoric for Writers* (HarperCollins 4th ed. 2001)

Matthew Butterick, *Typography for Lawyers: Essential Tools for Polished & Persuasive Documents* (Jones-McClure 2013)

Reed Dickerson, *The Fundamentals of Legal Drafting* (Little, Brown 1986)

Bryan A. Garner, *Legal Writing in Plain English* (Univ. Chicago Press 2d ed. 2013)

Bryan A. Garner, *The Winning Brief: 100 Tips for Persuasive Briefing in Trial and Appellate Courts* (Oxford Univ. Press 1999)

Joe Glaser, *Understanding Style: Practical Ways to Improve Your Writing* (Oxford Univ. Press 2009)

Ross Guberman, *Point Made: How to Write Like the Nation's Top Advocates* (Oxford Univ. Press 2d ed. 2014)

Verlyn Klinkenborg, *Several Short Sentences About Writing* (Knopf 2013)

Noah A. Messing, *The Art of Advocacy: Briefs, Motions, and Writing Strategies of America's Best Lawyers* (Wolters Kluwer 2013)

Tina L. Stark, *Drafting Contracts: How and Why Lawyers Do What They Do* (Aspen 2d ed. 2013)

John R. Trimble, *Writing with Style: Conversations on the Art of Writing* (Prentice Hall 2d ed. 2000)

Joseph M. Williams, *Style: Toward Clarity and Grace* (Univ. Chicago Press 1995)

Index

Founded in 1893,
UNIVERSITY OF CALIFORNIA PRESS
publishes bold, progressive books and journals
on topics in the arts, humanities, social sciences,
and natural sciences—with a focus on social
justice issues—that inspire thought and action
among readers worldwide.

The UC PRESS FOUNDATION
raises funds to uphold the press's vital role
as an independent, nonprofit publisher, and
receives philanthropic support from a wide
range of individuals and institutions—and from
committed readers like you. To learn more, visit
ucpress.edu/supportus.

Printed in the USA
CPSIA information can be obtained
at www.ICGtesting.com
CBHW031456220824
13472CB00014B/803